LIVING
WHOLE
WITHOUT A
BETTER HALF

Wendy Widder

kregel
PUBLICATIONS

Grand Rapids, MI 49501

To the Beldans *Thank you for your kind words & encouragement! Run the race!* *Wendy Widder* *Feb. 12:1-3*

Living Whole Without a Better Half

© 2000 by Wendy L. Widder

Published by Kregel Publications, a division of Kregel, Inc., P.O. Box 2607, Grand Rapids, MI 49501. For more information about Kregel Publications, visit our web site: www.kregel.com.

Library of Congress Cataloging-in-Publication Data
Widder, Wendy L.
   Living whole without a better half / by Wendy L. Widder
      p.   cm.
   1. Single people—Religious life. 2. Christian life—Biblical teaching. I. Title.
BV4596.S5 W53   2000   248.8'4—dc21   00-035731
                                             CIP

ISBN 0-8254-4111-0

Printed in the United States of America

1 2 3 4 5 / 04 03 02 01 00

*To Tammy,
my dear friend, beloved
roommate, and faithful
teammate. I couldn't have
run this stretch without you.*

Contents

Acknowledgments

$\mathcal{M}$y name may appear on the cover, but don't be fooled. Writing a book is a team effort. Without the advice, experiences, and encouragement of so many, the following pages would be blank. I could never create an exhaustive list of all who have had an impact on my writing, but I can thank the key players on the team:

Julie Ford—You were right. I should've written this book.

Glenn G.—Thanks for equipping me with the hardware, software, and expertise (computer and life) to make this project happen. I appreciate you.

Brent Gibbs—Thanks for finding me and agreeing that we had something to say. You made this happen.

Kerry M.—Thanks for letting me watch you learn how to run. I'm so glad to be on your team.

David—my coworker, pastor, boss, fan, editor, visionary, big brother, and forever friend. Thanks for believing in me.

Jeff and Julie—my friends for life. Thanks for honest words when I need them most, deep love that isn't dimmed by distance, and exemplary lives that challenge me to love Him more.

Mom and Dad—Thanks for being teachable as I've walked you through the truths about singleness. Thanks for learning what *not* to say! Thanks for years and years and years of silent, unshakable support. Thanks for laying a foundation in my life that invites God to build in His magnificent way. Thanks for, thanks for, thanks for . . .

Suzy—my sister, my friend. Thanks for reading and re-reading with your English-teacher eyes and red pen. Thanks for reading with a deep knowledge of and undying love for the author. *Your* words have been stickers of praise on my heart. I love you forever.

Jason—You have been the defining person of my adult life. God's indescribable plan included you, and, while I've sometimes wondered why, this book helps answer the question. You have been an example to me of running the race with eyes fixed straight ahead. May your feet never swerve from the only course that counts.

GBC family—You've been there from the cradle to college to careers one, two, three, and counting! Thank you for creating an environment where I could grow, and thank you for being a family I'll always love. I'm proud to call you "home."

GBC staff—You are the best team in the world. You stood around me when the hardest parts of being single overtook my life. You held my hands up when darkness threatened to swallow the victory God wanted to accomplish. You listened to each completed chapter and urged me on with your loving words. Our Monday mornings around a crowded staff table provided enough love, learning, and laughter to fill every day of every week. I've loved running with you!

CrossRoad—Truth be told, I really wanted to graduate from our class a *long* time ago! Being a "pillar" in the Garfield singles ministry was not something I planned. But God did, and I'm glad. Thanks for letting me stick around! And thanks for letting me practice what I preach in front of a live audience.

Tammy—What a ride! Thanks for *living* this book with me! I know you really don't need to read the following pages—you've heard them so often, you can practically recite them with me. God knew what He was doing when He put us together.

Introduction

$\mathcal{M}$aster of mystery Alfred Hitchcock once said, "The only way to get rid of my fears is to make films about them." That's the way I've felt about writing this book. Singleness is not something I dreamed about as a little girl. It was something I dreaded like an incurable disease, dooming me to a life of loneliness and despondency. It was something I prayed only happened to other people.

As my twenties edged closer to thirty and I found myself as single as it gets, my friend Julie Ford suggested I write a book about singleness. I laughed and thought that the last thing I wanted to do was become an "expert" on something I was wishing away like adolescent acne (with equivalent success). However, when a series of unwanted circumstances sent me deep into the dark valley of my fears, I discovered that God had an answer for every one of those fears. I found Him more than big enough to deal with what terrified me. Writing this book became a spiritual journey as God walked with me through the tough issues and emotions of singleness.

If you're single, I don't have to explain what those issues and emotions are. You live them. And you probably know what's on the bookshelves for us. I can't read another book about how to fix my "problem" of singleness. I don't want another person to tell me what I need to do while I'm "waiting" for a spouse to stumble into my life. I want to live the abundant life God promised with no marital strings attached. I want to make my one and only life matter for eternity, whether or not I ever walk down the aisle in white.

If you're *not* single, you know what those issues and emotions are, too. You also live them. "How can that be?" you ask. It's true, because the issues of singleness are not unique to spouseless people. They are really issues of fallen humanity. Loneliness. Unfulfilled desires. Unanswered questions. Pain. Rejection. Stubbornness. Commitment. Fear. Ill-placed priorities. While I write about these struggles from my own perspective as a single adult, the principles are the same for the circumstances that surround you.

Thanks for letting my world collide with yours for just a short time. It is my earnest prayer that God uses His truths and my words to help you love Him more tomorrow than you do today.

And They Lived Happily Ever After

*It's a snap to find the one single person in the world
who fills your heart with joy.*

—Joe Fox, *You've Got Mail*

*A*re you and Mrs. Pepper *friends?*"

The incredulous voice told me this was a revolutionary thought. My fifth grade student, like most of her classmates, thought she had a handle on what it meant to be a teacher. She knew, for example, that teachers get sadistic thrills from coloring papers red with ink. Teachers have insatiable appetites to bring offending students to swift judgment. Teachers spend most, if not all, of their allotted hours surrounded by creaky desks and dusty chalkboards.

Teachers don't understand Saturday morning cartoons. They don't go to the grocery store or the dry cleaners. They don't have any sympathy for what it's like to be ten years old, since it's unlikely they ever were. And for certain, teachers don't have friends.

My student learned a lesson I hadn't planned to teach her that day. Indeed, Mrs. Pepper and I were friends. For three years, Barb Pepper and I taught our fifth grade classes across the hall from each other, and we found ourselves captured in a rare relationship, a diamond of a friendship. We were "kindred spirits," as Anne of Green Gables would say. No detail was too trivial to share, no thought was too shocking to voice, no joke was too small to keep from the other.

During the last year we taught together, we exchanged notes and shared giggles as if we were a couple of schoolgirls ourselves. Barb was pregnant that year, and I was dating a man I thought I recognized from my dreams. We both were living at the pinnacle of excitement, one for new life and one for new love, and we had fun.

Somewhere between laughs and lessons, we talked about life, mostly mine. Barb was on a mission to get me married, and she was convinced I was halfway down the aisle already. I supported this belief in whatever ways I could, sharing the pertinent, as well as the absolutely irrelevant, details of my developing relationship.

Several months into the academic year, the fog in my dream lifted, and I realized I didn't know the man I was dating after all. We broke up, and Barb began her "bigger and better" campaign. "If we thought Tom was so wonderful, just imagine what *he* will be like." One particular day, Barb was carrying on in her familiar way. On this occasion, though, she added the oft-used Scripture verse about God giving you the desires of your heart as confirmation that I would definitely get married. Unsuspectingly, she had pulled a trigger and made herself the target of my speech about singleness.

"Where," I asked, "does the Bible promise that I'll get married? It doesn't. I know lots of singles, older than I, who have the desire in their hearts to be married, and they are not." I was just getting started, and as I lectured on, Barb felt like she'd unleashed a rabid dog!

I managed to reprogram Barb's thinking (or I scared her into silence!), and now she's careful to encourage without offering empty promises. But Barb is just a little droplet in a sea of people holding faulty assumptions about singleness.

Lie #1—God Is a Genie

One assumption is that God will give us what we want, just because we follow Him. Furthermore, He will do it in the way that we expect. It doesn't take a seminary degree to figure out that this is not true.

Like you, I have a lifelong list of "heart desires" that I never received. As a child, with all my heart I wanted a pet monkey. Mom wouldn't even entertain the idea. As an adolescent, I begged God for a clear complexion. Instead I got sick to my stomach taking tetracycline. As a teen, I wished to not have to ride the school bus with the elementary kids; by graduation, I was still riding the big yellow bus to school. As a collegian, I longed to meet "Mr. Right." Obviously, I'm still single. As a teacher, I longed for changed lives in wayward students, only to see them sink deeper in depravity.

God doesn't give us everything we deeply desire . . . The more significant truth is that He goes beyond our desires.

God doesn't give us everything we deeply desire. The truth is, He hears the cries of our hearts, and He does answer. But as God, He holds the right to answer His way. The more significant truth is that He goes *beyond* our desires.

Jesus recognized the real need and answered in His way, satisfying the deepest longing of the man's heart.

In his gospel, the apostle John tells the story of a man with an expressed desire that God chose to bypass. The fifth chapter opens at the Pool of Bethesda, a first-century nursing home for Jerusalem's down-and-outs. Admittedly, it may have been a home, but not much nursing took place around this pool. Medical treatment was only received by the first patient to get in the water when it periodically stirred. One very frustrated resident had been an invalid for thirty-eight years and had never won the race to the water. His real handicap, he said, was that he had no one to help him in the pool. If a roving reporter from the *Jerusalem Herald* had interviewed him, he would have issued a plea for someone to help him: "Just get me in the water."

His desire was close to coming true when Jesus visited the Bethesda Nursing Home. Jesus asked the question, "Do you want to get well?" Ignoring the obvious, *"Yes!"* the poolside patient uttered his deepest desire, "I just need someone to get me in the water."

Jesus didn't grant his desire. He did better. Instead of helping him in the water at the magical moment, Jesus recognized the real need and answered in His way, satisfying the deepest longing of the man's heart. He healed his body and offered healing for his soul. Jesus went beyond what the man thought to ask.

Jesus is not a bottle-bound genie summoned to grant every desire. He is, rather, an all-knowing, all-powerful, all-present Keeper of divine promises. And His list of promises is more than impressive. It's overwhelming.

> {He} satisfies your desires with good things so that your youth is renewed like the eagle's.
>
> —Psalm 103:5

> No good thing does he withhold from those whose walk is blameless.
>
> —Psalm 84:11b

> My God will meet all your needs according to his glorious riches in Christ Jesus.
>
> —Philippians 4:19

> My grace is sufficient for you, for my power is made perfect in weakness.
>
> —2 Corinthians 12:9

> And we know that in all things God works for the good of those who love him, who have been called according to his purpose.
>
> —Romans 8:28

Perhaps *my* definition of these fulfilled promises is a spouse, but God and I often have different ideas about the way my life should be. My 20/20 hindsight leaves no doubt that His ideas are always better than mine.

Lie #2—Singleness Is Second-Rate

A second false assumption says that to not be married is to miss out on the best in life. Being single means being short-changed.

When I was in college, I did a fair job of attending classes regularly. At times, however, I weighed my options and class attendance lost. This occurred frequently during the winter quarter of my sophomore year. By then, as a declared education major, I was taking some classes that applied directly to education. One such class was scheduled for two o'clock every afternoon for ten weeks. The focus of the class was something like "effective assessment of student learning."

It took me two weeks to figure out that if I attended class on Monday, I'd get the bulk of the week's notes. Tuesday through Friday were spent in laborious explanation and application of Monday's concepts. By the third week, I'd established my routine: attend class every Monday, pop in on Wednesday or Thursday to catch up, and carefully follow the test schedule.

One of the skills we spent too many days working on was test writing, being able to accurately assess student learning. Dr. Andrews taught us how to write multiple choice tests that didn't scream obvious answers; he taught us how to glean the most information from essay questions; and he taught us about matching tests—you know, the kind with twenty questions or words that must be correctly matched with the twenty choices.

Dr. Andrews was insistent that a good test always has *more* options than needed. This helps prevent students from getting answers right simply because there are no other choices. There should be a handful of answers left over, unmatched.

Sometimes it seems that God has written a cosmic matching test, pairing men and women with each other. And, true to effective test writing, He's included some extra answers, options that don't really fit on the test. Without the other half, they are incomplete. They are missing something.

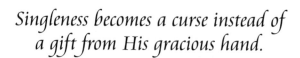

Singleness becomes a curse instead of a gift from His gracious hand.

An Age-Old Lie

In these two faulty assumptions, Satan has rephrased the lie of Eden: "If you are single, you are missing something wonderful. God can't be good if He withholds something so desirable." Like Eve, we ponder the lie, and given space, it settles in. It begins its insidious mission, robbing us of God's richest gifts. We entertain the thought that God is unfair, withholding marriage for no good reason. Singleness becomes a curse instead of a gift from His gracious hand. Being alone is a cross we must bear instead of a powerful position He can use. And while we'd never admit it, we doubt Him. Like Eve, we then set about the task of making God's plan fit into our plan. We focus energy on solving the problem of our singleness, going in search of God's "better gift," marriage.

Running the Right Race

My church, like most across the country, runs a week of vacation Bible school for kids every summer. Several years ago, our program centered on a kids' musical entitled "G. T. and the Halo Express: Winning the Great Race of Faith." The story followed a group of children competing in a bike race. A flat tire, a huge hill, a tired teammate, and a big bad bully named Billy Baxter nearly eliminated the group from the contest. Midway through the race, the map they were following seemed wrong, and they narrowly escaped getting off course. Crisis after crisis bombarded the team, but they managed to press on to the finish line and win.

Much of their encouragement during the race came from a host of singing angels, the Halo Express. Bible verses set to music provided just the right words at just the right times. The theme verse, Hebrews 12:1, set the tone for the entire race. "Therefore, since we are surrounded by such a great cloud of witnesses, let us throw off everything that hinders and the sin that so easily entangles, *and let us run with perseverance the race marked out for us*" (emphasis mine).

The last part of this verse, especially, offered three encouragements to the weary bikers. First of all, the race was marked out; simply follow the map. Secondly, persevere; things will definitely be tough, but you can do it. And finally, run; keep moving forward and give it all the energy you have. It was a recipe for success in the bike race, but it's also a pretty clear formula for success in life, especially as a single adult. It's the truth that combats Satan's lie.

My race has been marked out. I must follow God's map. Right now the course has me running solo. Maybe a teammate will join me around the next bend, but maybe not. I just don't know the terrain of God's established route.

Persevere—things will definitely be tough. There will be loneliness, rejection, and uncertainty. There will be difficulties unique to singleness. Press on anyway.

And perhaps most importantly—run. This race demands

the best energies I can give. I can't afford to meander along the course, looking around for a better route. I have to quit waiting for life to happen to me. This course requires pro-active living—setting my sights and running.

Hearing the Right Crowd

I'm not the first one to run a tough race and neither are you. In fact, welcome to the *human* race! I take comfort in the expression, "There's nothing new under the sun," knowing that billions of people have run before me. (If that doesn't put life in perspective, nothing will!) They've "been there, done that." They serve as witnesses that life's circumstances aren't intended to ruin the race; they *are* the race. Their stories are swigs of cold water to sweaty athletes; their examples are splashes of refreshment to weary runners.

I'm not much of an athlete, but in recent years, I've developed a passion for the game of football (strictly as a spectator). During a season when I dated a footballaholic, I joined the Wisconsin masses and became an official cheesehead, a Green Bay Packer fan. Growing up in America's Dairyland during the Packers' less-than-glory years, I had always been indifferent toward a team that changed head coaches and quarterbacks faster than I lost my baby teeth. But in 1994, the Packers were on the rise. Quarterback Brett Favre put the entire state of Wisconsin on the edges of their couches from week to week, wondering if he would throw more interceptions or touchdowns. Fans fell in love with a big teddy bear of a player on a mission to wear a Super Bowl ring, "The Minister of Defense," Reggie White.

Every Packer fan knows that a pilgrimage to Lambeau Field to watch the green and gold in action is like winning

the lottery. With a season ticket waiting list longer than
Santa's, getting to a game is a wild dream fans never expect to come true. Unbelievably, I managed to win the lottery one Monday night, and with three friends, I made the
semi-sacred journey to Green Bay for a game against the
Philadelphia Eagles. Driving into Title Town, it was obvious that the entire town had the game on its schedule. Entrepreneurs lined the sidewalks in their lawn chairs, selling
space in their front yards for parking. Local businesses
boasted their team's prowess on exterior signs. Swarms of
sweatshirted ticket holders paraded toward the Midwest-
ern Mecca. Cars filled with hooting Packer-maniacs crawled
into the stadium lot. Approaching the stadium, we walked
through the haze of grill smoke and declined several offers
of bratwurst, the official food of Packer fans. Once inside
Lambeau, we were surrounded by fans intoxicated with their
team's success (and a lot of something else, too). From overhead, the Goodyear® blimp filmed a party sixty thousand
strong.

When the players finally broke into the field's light, the
crowd erupted. With banners waving and arms flailing, the
fans cheered their beloved Packers. Reflecting the crowd's
enthusiasm, the team charged through their warm-up, as
if to say, "We dare anyone to beat us here." And most teams
don't. The electrified fans create an environment antago-
nistic to opponents.

But there's more to historic Lambeau Field than a crazed
crowd. The stadium itself is a modern-day shrine. Names
like Bart Starr, Vince Lombardi, Curly Lambeau, Don
Hutson, and Ray Nitscke surround the stadium. They are
mounted as reminders to say, "This is the home of winners.
We are unmatched in NFL history. Read our names and
remember. Remember what we did. You can do it, too."

It's an ever present beckoning to be better, an invitation to excel. Some perfervid fans even allege that the "spirit of Vince" roams the stadium, driving the present players as he did their forerunners.

Except for the part about Vince, this is the sort of picture I get when I read about the "great cloud of witnesses" in Hebrews 12:1. The author issues a challenge to any who will take it. Referring back to chapter eleven, he says, "See the names all around you? They did it and so can you." Names of men and women who have gone on before and overcome. Names of men and women who faced life head-on and prevailed.

I've read enough biographies to know that some of my fellow sojourners reach the end and say, "I fought a good fight, I finished the course, I won the prize." Then there are those who reach the end and admit, "I missed the fight, I fought the course, I never saw the prize."

Telling story upon story of their faith, the author makes his methodical way through early Old Testament history. He paints pictures of the obvious celebrities like Abraham, Isaac, and Jacob, and then sketches in some obscure characters like Enoch, Amram, and Jochebed. Etched under each portrait is a tribute to great faith. It's not a nebulous, warm-fuzzy faith; it's a "no-holds-barred" aggressive faith. It's an unexplained certainty in the unseen, and it spurs the faith-holder to action. This kind of faith received God's commendation and inscribed their names in the annals of biblical history. Their lives serve as inspiration to us. They are swigs of cold water and splashes of refreshment.

As nice and noble as that may sound, the truth of the matter is that seeing their names and knowing their stories are not enough. Playing football in the legendary Lambeau Field during the 1970s and 1980s certainly didn't earn the pathetic Packers any titles. It takes more than history to change the present and the future.

Traveling the Light Way

When I was in junior high, my favorite teacher was a fresh-out-of-college novice who brought more to class than a lesson plan and a list of assignments. Mr. Moore liked to have fun, and with his seventh graders that included spending our free time in jacks tournaments, table tennis matches, and a runners' club. I learned how to play jacks and I thrived on table tennis, but I am not a runner. However, when my favorite teacher challenged me to run fifty miles in five weeks, I groaned and signed up in spite of my abhorrence for the activity.

Every night I tied my tattered laces and started down the block toward Center Street, the halfway point where I would turn around and pant for home. I hated every block of the six hundred I ran in those five weeks. I tried singing in my head, breathing rhythmically, varying my pace, all to no avail. Nothing made it any more enjoyable. Nothing made it any easier.

I do know what would have made it harder, though. Carrying my backpack with all the homework I hauled home from seventh grade would have killed me. Running with that weight, I never would have made those nightly twelve blocks. If I had run with my double-knotted shoelaces untied, I never would have made it either; I would have fallen before I finished. Running with such a hindering weight or entanglement would have left me confined to the curb or sprawled on the sidewalk.

Hebrews 12:1 doesn't claim that being surrounded by such a great host of examples is enough. In fact, it's really just the beginning. The Hebrews 11 cast of characters proved it can be done, and now I've got to do it. For starters, I've got to throw off everything that hinders and get rid of the sin that so easily entangles. Only then can I run.

There are a lot of Christians confined to the curb or sprawled on the sidewalk. Entangled by sin or just hindered by baggage, they are stuck. They've stopped running. They are sitting on the side, and I think a lot of them are single. Some are defeated by weights of loneliness and rejection, or stuck in sins of self-sufficiency and stubbornness. For others, the death of their dreams has halted their race. And still others are sidelined by laziness or lethargy.

Whatever the weight, whatever the sin, it's time to quit looking at the pebbles around our feet. Look up. See the names. Remember their faith. You can do it, too. Get up. Get back in the race. Running a race *is* hard work. Pressing on when you want to quit *is* excruciating. Believing that the race is sovereignly designed *is* difficult to swallow sometimes.

I've read enough biographies to know that some of my fellow sojourners reach the end and say, "I fought a good fight, I finished the course, I won the prize." Then there are those who reach the end and admit, "I missed the fight, I fought the course, I never saw the prize."

Lambeau Field is a hall of football fame, enshrining the greats of the game. I will never achieve Packer celebrity status. I don't have the skill, experience, or qualifications. Hebrews 11 is a memorial to men and women just like me. They faced the same weights and sins that I do. They fought the fight and ran the assigned course, and they made it. They won the prize.

So can I, and so can you, single friend. It's time to quit looking for something "better." It's time to throw off entanglements and sins. The pages of life keep turning, and some of us are stuck on the table of contents wondering where the marriage chapter is. We're missing the story.

Abraham: Living in the Unknown

You know it's easier to be killed by a terrorist than it is to get married over the age of forty.

—*Sleepless in Seattle*

*W*hen I finally moved out on my own, the staples of my diet became boxed macaroni and cheese, frozen vegetables, and canned soup. This was not a decision of dietary preference; it was a matter of cooking convenience. Concocting a "real meal" for one person is usually more hassle than it's worth. Occasionally, though, another instant meal is more than I can stomach, and I shuffle through my dusty collection of favorite Widder recipes. Often I pick one of my grandma's recipes from the assortment. Grandma Widder was a great cook. Her cooking was simple, but always good.

Over the years, her recipes have made their way through

the ranks of Widders, but the buck of success stops in my kitchen. My grandma knew some things she didn't tell. Most of her recipes read like a book with pages missing. "Add milk. Stir. Layer in pan. Cook until done." The absence of information frustrates a culinary novice such as I. For instance, I think it's helpful to know the recommended pan size. I also like to know exactly how much milk to add. And it seems to me that oven temperature and baking time are pertinent pieces of data. Grandma didn't need these things written out. She knew. Her dinners and desserts always turned out. For the expert, certain bits of information are simply understood. For the ignorant, those same bits of information are critical.

Missing Information

My grandma's recipes are somewhat analogous to Abraham's story. Major steps in the patriarch's life were punctuated by question marks; recipes for God's blessing seemed to be missing ingredients. In Hebrews 11, Abraham appears in eight verses, making him the most mentioned hero of Old Testament faith. Two simple words crowd their way into those verses three different times: "even though."

> *By faith Abraham, when called to go to a place . . . obeyed and went,* even though *he did not know where he was going.*
>
> —Hebrews 11:8 (emphasis mine)

> *By faith Abraham,* even though *he was past age . . . was enabled to become a father.*
>
> —Hebrews 11:11 (emphasis mine)

*By faith Abraham . . . offered Isaac as a sacrifice. . . .
even though God had said to him, "It is through Isaac
that your offspring will be reckoned."*

—Hebrews 11:17–18 (emphasis mine)

At crossroad moments in Abraham's life, God pulled back
the veil, revealing parts of His divine plan. He issued commands and bestowed promises. But when pulling back the
veil, it sometimes seems He covered Abraham's eyes. He
kept some vital pieces of information from Abraham. He
left some major questions unanswered. "Where am I going? How can that happen? When will You answer? Why
would You do this?" Yet Abraham followed. By faith the
Genesis patriarch lived in the midst of the unknown.

*I don't think Abraham really cared where on
earth he ended up.*

Where?

*By faith Abraham, when called to go to a place he
would later receive as his inheritance, obeyed and went,
even though he did not know where he was going. By
faith he made his home in the promised land like a
stranger in a foreign country; he lived in tents, as did
Isaac and Jacob, who were heirs with him of the same
promise. For he was looking forward to the city with
foundations, whose architect and builder is God.*

—Hebrews 11:8–10 (emphasis mine)

One September, a friend and I mapped out a road rally for our singles group. We drove through the autumn-streaked countryside, counting miles, tracking turns, and noting details. We wrote careful directions, step-by-step instructions for each car to follow. No one was told the final destination; that was the challenge. Groups that meticulously followed the route, noticed the landmarks, and stayed within speed limits arrived right on time for dinner. Other groups ignored the directions, blazed their own trail, and ended up frustrated and hungry.

God sent Abraham and his caravan on the ultimate road rally. "Go to a land I will show you." Without a clue where he was going, Abraham picked up the map and moved. His faith told him that God had planned the route. He had formed the landmarks and marked the miles, and He would determine the speed. Blindly, Abraham kept his camels moving toward an unknown piece of earth.

How could he do this? I'll tell you how. I don't think he really cared where on earth he ended up. Abraham's secret was knowing where *beyond* earth he'd end up. He had his compass pointed toward a city with eternal foundations, not a tent with moveable stakes. His destination was designed and built by God, and Abraham willingly forfeited all that was familiar to get there.

How? When?

> By faith Abraham, even though *he was past age—and Sarah herself was barren—was enabled to become a father because he considered him faithful who had made the promise. And so from this one man, and he as good as dead, came descendants as numerous as the stars in the sky and as countless as the sand on the seashore.*
>
> —Hebrews 11:11–12 (emphasis mine)

If ever a man was in the place to ask God "How?" it was Abraham. Part of God's promise in Genesis 12 was to make Abraham into a great nation. God went on to promise a parcel of land to Abraham's offspring. There were several problems with this promise, beginning with the fact that Abraham didn't have any offspring. To make matters worse, Abraham was approaching his centennial birthday. Perhaps most critically, Abraham's wife was barren. How could God make him the father of a nation when Abraham couldn't even become the father of a son? It's one thing for God to leave out ingredients or directions; it's entirely different to include ingredients that are impossible to obtain.

Amazingly, we don't hear Abraham ask any questions until chapter 15, but by then, he is not asking "How?" Abraham knew his God was powerful; he knew He could do what He had promised—somehow. God's plan no longer shocked him; what did plague him, though, was "When?"

> *O Sovereign Lord, what can you give me since I remain childless? . . . You have given me no children.*
>
> —Genesis 15:2–3

God took His time fulfilling promises to Abraham. Isaac, the son of promise, wasn't born until twenty-five years after God first spoke. Twenty-five years of waiting. This act of faith involved no commands to obey, only a promise to believe. For twenty-five years, Abraham trusted God to be faithful. I'm sure he was frustrated and impatient a day or two out of the 9,125. And I'm sure he sent cries of desperation heavenward in moments of despair. To be sure, he had his moments of doubt, skepticism, and even attempts to help God, but the prevailing theme of Abraham's life is that he trusted God.

What Abraham didn't know was that in those two and a half dark decades of waiting, God slowly conditioned his faith, working it into shape for an even bigger test to come.

Why?

> *By faith Abraham, when God tested him, offered Isaac as a sacrifice. He who had received the promises was about to sacrifice his one and only son,* even though God had said to him, "It is through Isaac that your offspring will be reckoned."
>
> —Hebrews 11:17–18 (emphasis mine)

Just when Abraham's biography got to the page that should have read "and they lived happily ever after," God added another chapter, the most painful yet. Isaac had erased decades of pain with his first cry, and he brought years of long-awaited laughter to his elderly parents. Abraham and Sarah enjoyed every stage of Isaac's childhood. Too quickly he outgrew bouncing on Abraham's knees, and too soon he stopped bringing Sarah fistfuls of wilted weeds. The son of promise, the heir of God's blessing, grew up.

Abraham didn't have to know the answer—he knew the Antidote. He knew God could fix it.

Then Abraham became the victim of an apparent cruel, cosmic joke when God asked the unfathomable. "Take your son, your only son Isaac, whom you love, and . . . sacrifice him as a burnt offering." Why would God ask such a thing? Why would a father be told to kill his son? Why would God make and fulfill promises to Abraham, only to negate them later? Why would God allow Abraham the joy of Isaac and then inflict such pain? There are a thousand "whys" to God's ultimate command to Abraham.

Yet the Bible doesn't tell us that Abraham asked any of them. Instead, we know that by faith Abraham offered Isaac. By faith he raised a knife over the bound body of his boy. By faith he prepared to slay his son. When Isaac asked his father, "Where is the lamb for the burnt offering?" Abraham answered, "God Himself will provide the lamb." Did you ever wonder what Abraham said when Isaac, atop the altar, looked into his father's eyes, flooded with anguish, and with his own eyes asked, "Dad, why?"

Hebrews 11 gives the only answer Abraham had for his bewildered son, and his bewildered self, too. "Abraham reasoned that God could raise the dead" (v. 19). When swimming in a sea of "whys," Abraham trusted in the power of God. He didn't have to know the answer—he knew the Antidote. He knew God could fix it.

Someone has described faith as seeing the invisible, believing the incredible, and receiving the impossible. Abraham's life was marked by significant questions for which God offered no answers. Yet Abraham didn't demand answers. Instead, by faith he saw what no one else did, believed what no one else could, and received what no one else would.

Isn't It About Time You Got Married?

I live millennia from Genesis and miles from the Promised Land, but I've got a few unanswered questions about

my life, too. I'd like to know if I'll ever get rich and famous from this book. I'd like to know if I'll ever be a home-
maker and homeowner. I'd like to know how to sell and
buy, as well as manage maintenance on, a car as a single
woman. I'd like to know if I'll ever walk down the aisle as
the main attraction instead of as a member of the support-
ing cast. I've discovered, though, that I rarely have to ask
questions like this. There are plenty of other people in my
life asking them for me.

*After wrestling repeatedly with these
and other questions about singleness,
I've resigned myself to the fact that God is the
only One who knows the answers,
and He's not telling.*

At a church event one evening, I was serving punch,
stocking cookie trays, and cleaning up messes, when a mere
acquaintance asked one. Punch ladle in hand, attention fo-
cused on stirring pink sherbet, I heard his voice. "So, isn't
it about time you got married?" Glancing left and right
with the desperate hope that he was speaking to *anyone* else,
I slowly looked up. Nope, I was the lucky target, and he
hit the bull's-eye.

"Isn't it about time you got married?" He voiced one of those
questions that lurks in the heart of every single adult who
desires to be married. It resides next to half a dozen others
we've been asked over the years—questions for which we
either don't have the answers or don't like the answers:

- Do you have a boyfriend?
- You're a nice girl; why aren't you dating anyone?
- How's your love life? [Would you dare ask a married person this?!]
- Are you looking for a husband?
- So, you're still single?
- Do you *want* to get married?

If you are single, you've fielded most of these and countless other remarks for which any answer seems inadequate. You've probably mastered the courtesy laugh and polite smile, and chances are you're an expert at shifting conversations away from your marital status.

While I laugh at both well-meaning friends and rude acquaintances for asking such bold things, they are really only voicing questions I have in my own head. I just don't ask them because I know there aren't answers. *If* I'll marry, *who* I'll marry, *when* I'll marry, are some of God's question marks in my life, unknown obstacles in my race. That's the way God planned it. After wrestling repeatedly with these and other questions about singleness, I've resigned myself to the fact that God is the only One who knows the answers, and He's not telling. Most days I can live with that. Not everybody in my life has struggled through these issues, though, and so for them, I sometimes just don't fit into a preconceived mold.

Working the Puzzle

One of my sisters is an expert puzzler. Unlike my dad, who likes to dump all the pieces on the table, Bonnie prefers to hold the box in one hand and stir through it with the other, looking for certain pieces. When she strikes, she's rarely wrong. Her practiced eye knows where pieces fit without even trying them. I love puzzles, too, and while I learned much of my skill from watching Bonnie, I can't compete with her prowess. I have a knack for picking a piece that *looks* like it should fit, but no matter how many times I try, it doesn't. I turn it and try again. Nope. I set it down in the corner of the board and when I come back to it, I think all over again that it *must* fit in *that* place. Like a dull-witted dog chasing parked cars, I keep putting the same right piece in the same wrong place. It makes no sense to me—how a piece with the right coloring and the right shape just doesn't fit.

To married friends and relatives, singles are sometimes those puzzle pieces. It looks to them as if we should fit in a certain place. In attempts to make us fit, they often ask bold questions. At times they answer their own questions when our responses fall short of what they hoped to hear:

- God has someone very special for you.
- You just wait—your day is coming.
- You'll make somebody a perfect wife.
- He just doesn't know what he's missing.
- You never know who you'll meet.
- I hope you meet someone special; I really want you to be happy.

Begging the forgiveness of my friends and family, I don't have nearly as many problems with the unanswered *questions* in my life as I do with their *answers!* I wholeheartedly recognize their good intentions. They never mean to be invasive or rude; they really want only the best for me. I love them for it, and I've learned to laugh at them for it, too.

Like I said, most days I can live with God's absence of answers. But sometimes, I allow myself to listen to the well-meaning advice of bystanders, and I choose to hear their answers above the silence of God. When I filter their pieces of intended encouragement through my emotional sieve, I want to believe them. I want to take their statements as divine wisdom.

Maybe time will prove their words correct in my life, but I can't afford to live with that expectation. If I do, chances are good I will park myself on the side of the road or hoist a heavy bag over my shoulder and squander this leg of the race.

Learning to Let Go

When I moved into my apartment, it pained me to un-pack my brand-new dishes and actually use them . . . by myself. For several years, I had amassed a collection of dishes for my hope chest, and they, along with several other boxes of household items, were not intended to be used until I got married. Opening the boxes and unwrapping each piece was a solemn occasion, as I let go of some long-held dreams.

We are faced with two choices:
pull over and wait for our self-scripted lives to
catch up, or forget the plan and focus on the
road ahead.

I recently talked to a friend in the middle of the "all my friends are getting married" phase, and she mourned her place in life. She talked of the many things she thought she'd be doing at this point—with her husband. To go ahead and do them without him seemed like an admission of defeat, admitting all of her dreams were dead.

Most of us grew up expecting to graduate from high school, go to college, get married, start a family, and then turn twenty-five. For many of us, though, we're racing toward twenty-five with no prospects on the horizon, or we're looking at twenty-five in the rearview mirror with no one else in the car. We are faced with two choices: pull over and wait for our self-scripted lives to catch up, or forget the plan and focus on the road ahead.

Some singles do their best to focus on the road ahead, carrying lists of adventures to have and goals to achieve. They busily check things off alone, but nagging deep inside is a disappointment with the way life has turned out. Unfulfilled expectations have planted seeds of discontent. The grass looks greener on the other side of "I do," and being single is a phase to endure until true happiness whisks them over the fence.

For them, singles' activities become "hunting grounds." Side-glances intimate true love, and small conversations are laden with significant undercurrents. Sometimes we call them "desperate," but desperate is just a symptom of a deeper issue—discontentment. You don't have to be in the same company long to know they're unhappy and dissatisfied. It's heard in their cynical statements; it's seen on their faces. God's course isn't what they want; singleness wasn't their plan. The weight of discontent drains their joy.

They think what's missing is the joy of a relationship and marriage. Ironically, what's really missing is joy in general— joy of life, joy of singleness. I can hear the skeptical laugh of some single friends—"Joy of singleness?!" Yup. If there's not joy in singleness, there won't be joy in marriage either. Joy is not the fruit of "favorable" circumstances. Rather, it's the outpouring of a contented heart.

Cultivating Contentment

Content. The root of the word means "contained." Dr. Warren Wiersbe says it describes a "man whose resources are within him so that he does not have to depend on substitutes without."[1] It's the portrait of a person who withstands the blows of life by drawing upon what's inside. New Agers would applaud such a statement, but the truth is that only God supplies such internal resources. God *in* us provides more than an adequate supply of spiritual strength.

*The secret of contentment
begins with acknowledging that
God is sovereign and that
God is sufficient.*

Philippians is a book penned by a man buffeted by life's bad weather, but yet a man with a contented heart. Eugene Peterson calls the epistle "infectiously happy." "Before we've read a dozen lines, we begin to feel the joy ourselves—the dance of words and the exclamations of delight have a way of getting inside us."[2] Joy spills from Paul's pen across the pages of his letter; it's drenched with obvious contentment and confidence. Perhaps Paul was just one of those annoying people who actually wakes up when the alarm goes off. Instead of stumbling in *and* out of the shower, maybe he had his day half planned before the water ever got hot. It's possible he whistled while preparing breakfast and then finished a few household tasks before strolling off to work.

His personality could have been a factor, but Paul makes it clear that he didn't come by contentment and joy strictly through genetics. He *learned* it, and he learned it the hard way: ". . . for I have learned to be content whatever the circumstances" (Phil. 4:11). His list of circumstances stacks up against anybody's claim to hardship: he'd been imprisoned, flogged, exposed, beaten with rods, stoned until nearly dead, and shipwrecked three times. Everywhere he went—city, country, open seas—he was in danger. His enemies included bandits, his own countrymen, Gentiles, and false brothers. He had gone without food and water; he had known cold and nakedness. Oh, and one more thing—he was probably single.

Paul took life's tests and aced them. Adversities became the objects of growth that God intended them to be. How could he so happily endure such hardship? Near the end of Philippians, Paul reveals that he had learned the "secret of being content in any and every situation" (4:12). The cheat sheet for the secret is found throughout his writings. Paul knew above all else that God was sovereign. God was in control. When the ship became floating debris or dear coworkers forsook the gospel, God had a plan. Secondly, Paul had confidence that God was sufficient. He trusted God's ability to work His plan. God's power *in* Paul was more than enough to handle any circumstance. "I can do everything through him who gives me strength" (4:13). The secret of contentment, then, begins with acknowledging that God is sovereign and that God is sufficient. The secret is sealed, however, when experience proves it true.

Enjoying the Ride

My favorite joyful person talks with a southern Indiana accent. He's a Hoosier to the bone with basketball in his blood and a grin that's permanently stretched across his face. His laughter splashes joy across any room.

Jon McDugle is a year younger than I, but he's seen a lot more of life than I have. More accurately, he's come face-to-face with death more than I have. During his first week at college, Jon's mom was diagnosed with cancer. After a two-year struggle, she died. After graduation, Jon married his high school sweetheart, Tammy, and headed to seminary. During their time in seminary, Tammy was diagnosed with cancer. She won the five-month battle, but not before Jon put his educational and career plans on hold.

When Jon finally approached graduation from seminary, he candidated at my church for the position of youth pastor. He went through hours of interviews and meetings that would put an FBI investigation to shame, answering an endless stream of questions about his philosophy of youth ministry and how he intended to implement it. I, along with the rest of those who listened to him, recognized his enthusiasm and obvious gifts for ministry, but also hesitated slightly at his inexperience.

Yet there was something about Jon that made his professional experience less important. Jon had experience with life and with God. He had faced a series of the most difficult pitches life can throw, and he had swung the bat of God's sovereignty and sufficiency. I never doubted that Jon could do the job we were calling him to do, because in addition to his gifts and passions, he had the inner resources to do any job. He had learned the secret of contentment.

Of all the things Jon said during that weekend of

candidating, one statement is imprinted in my memory. It came in response to a parent's question about how he would handle difficult situations. Jon answered that his goal was to view every problem as an adventure and to enjoy the ride. That's joy. Joy that comes from a confident contentment in God. In his own words, Jon desires to be "ever-saturated with the sufficiency of God." Dr. Wiersbe calls this kind of living being the victor instead of the victim.[3]

It's easy to want to be the victim. Life isn't fair, and it often doesn't make sense. It is full of unanswered questions and uncomfortable answers. But the secret to enjoying it to its fullest, whatever "it" may be, is found in being content. Contentment keeps the statements of well-meaning friends from rattling you. It stills your reeling emotions when others make their journeys across the threshold. It grants peace when heaven is silent about your future. It turns Satan's attempts to defeat you into God's opportunities to amaze you.

3

Job: Living in Spite of Pain

*First, I remember being with my dad. He would get
these far off looks in his eye and he would say, "Life
doesn't always turn out the way you planned it." I just
wish I'd realized at the time he was talking about my
life.*

—Lucy, *While You Were Sleeping*

*E*verybody loves a good story. Children, especially, love a
tale with a very bad villain and a very big hero. Bible stories are blueprinted for little people, giving account after
account of God's chosen heroes prevailing over the forces
of evil itself. A child hearing the stories of Jonah and the
whale, Noah and the ark, Daniel in the lions' den, David
and Goliath, wishes to don dusty sandals and live in ancient tents. Old Testament champions of the faith come to
life in childish imaginations: pudgy fingers get tangled in

the bushy manes of hungry lions; little hearts skip beats when fire falls from heaven upon command; chubby arms pluck the gates of enemy cities like bothersome weeds. As adults, while we may not experience the childish thrill of vicariously living Old Testament stories, most of us would still like to see God do such amazing things through our feeble lives.

Job's suffering wasn't a cosmic "oops"; it was orchestrated by a sovereign God.

There is one biblical character, however, that I've never heard anyone, child or adult, long to be. He was noble, upright, blameless, and God-fearing. Like Abraham, he was wealthy and influential. In fact, he was the greatest man among the people of his time. Yet no one wants to trade places with him. No one wants to take the time machine to the doorstep of Job. He's not mentioned in Hebrews 11, but Job stands as history's hallmark of suffering and pain.

Job was blindsided by tragedy after tragedy until all he held dear was gone. His children, his health, his livelihood were all snatched from him. Job was left on a heap of ashes, scraping himself with bits of broken pottery. Then, as if the circumstantial suffering was not enough, Job was ambushed by three friends who talked too much, felt too little, and misunderstood everything. The most amazing part of the story, though, is that God allowed it. Job's suffering wasn't a cosmic "oops"; it was orchestrated by a sovereign God.

Job's story pulls us into a world where suffering is no respecter of persons, no discriminator based on marital status. No amount of money, prestige, or happiness cushioned Job from the onslaught of life-jarring events, and it won't protect us either. This is a world where God permits pain and tragedy to invade our lives, whether we are married or single. Singles face the pain of rejection, disappointment, loneliness, and the death of dreams. While it may be packaged differently, I'm sure married couples face the exact same kinds of pain. The circumstances differ, the intensity varies, and the frequency fluctuates from person to person, but sorrow is inevitable. If it hasn't barged into your world yet, enjoy the present calm, but know the storm will come. It'll come without your invitation. It may crash through the door and send you reeling, like it did for Job, or it may seep steadily under the door, like the slowly rising tide. Regardless, it will come and when it does, it might stay for a while.

Pain and a Cosmic Battle

Perhaps the most significant truth about pain is disclosed in the opening chapters of Job. In a succession of dialogues between God and Satan, the reality that human life is not confined to this planet becomes clear. Job's life took on cosmic proportions, involving the prince of this world and the King of eternity. His struggles were not the result of bad fortune, bad investments, or bad behavior. He was not simply the victim of a Russian roulette game of hardship. If anything, his suffering was the result of *righteous* living. God the Creator and Satan the Destroyer discussed Job, and the demolition of his life was the result. With God's permission, Satan stripped Job of nearly everything.

Job missed out on this conversation; he just lived through

the fallout. We, however, are privy to the dialogue between light and dark. Scripture records that one day the angels presented themselves to God, and Satan tagged along. Asked where he'd come from, Satan responded that he'd been roaming the earth. First Peter 5:8 informs us what is always behind satanic roaming: "Your enemy the devil prowls around like a roaring lion looking for someone to devour." In the next statement of this celestial conversation, it appears that God served up a choice servant for the Devil to devour. God's question, "Have you considered my servant Job? There is no one on earth like him; he is blameless and upright, a man who fears God and shuns evil" (Job 1:8), placed Job on a platter within lunging distance of the hellish beast.

Satan's response was nothing short of a demonic "Duh," as he accused God of giving Job everything he could possibly want and then some. "Who *wouldn't* be on Your side?" the Devil essentially asked. Satan issued the challenge for God to slap Job instead of stretching out His hand full of blessings. "Then we'll see what he's really made of," was his dare.

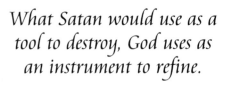

*What Satan would use as a
tool to destroy, God uses as
an instrument to refine.*

God's reply makes me shudder, "Very well, then, everything he has is in your hands" (Job 1:12), and Job's life was shredded as the Infinite faced off with the archenemy on a cosmic battleground. As sobering as this exchange between

God and the Devil is, there is a significant point to isolate. Don't overlook who's in control. He may be the prince of this world, but Satan does not lay a finger on God's children without God's permission. In all of Job's suffering, God never relinquished His authority over the events of Job's life.

Pain and a New Perspective

Like Job, my race has been marked out by God. Every obstacle in the path exists at His allowance. Every hill and each deep valley has been charted by Him. Much of the difficulty in the course is there because Satan has something to prove, and God has some*one* to prove. Job 23:10 declares that "he knows the way that I take; when he has tested me, I will come forth as gold."

Knowing that pain lays the turf for a cosmic battle puts a whole new feature on the face of suffering. What Satan would use as a tool to destroy, God uses as an instrument to refine. God longs for the difficult circumstances to strengthen my faith. He may never answer my cries of "why?" I may never understand the reasons for my singleness, and I may not see many results from my difficulties. Yet I know that each pain-laden skirmish in life is part of a grander battle. Pain spreads fertile soil for seeds of faith to grow. My faith begins to take root as I traverse through tough circumstances. I learn to hear and see God in ways I never could before pain invaded my life.

Comparatively speaking, I've lived a fairly charmed life. I grew up with two parents who deeply love God, each other, and their four children. I never struggled in school, I always felt loved by my teachers, and I usually had a collection of loyal friends. To be sure, I struggled through the stages of growing up and encountered some sizable bumps in the road, but all in all, my life has had a fairly straight and flat course. I grew up learning how to love God and learning to trust Him no matter what. However, I didn't encounter a definitive "no matter what" situation until I was twenty-seven.

I've not dated much in my life. With fingers left over, I can count my significant dating relationships on one hand. After years in the dating desert, God chose to surprise me. Jay was everything I'd ever put on a list and more. He exceeded my wildest dreams, and I had some wild ones. He went beyond my highest expectations, and I had some high ones. He was easily what no one else had ever been, or what I was sure nobody else could ever be. And wonder of wonders, he loved me.

Life was on a long-awaited track. It wasn't a perfect track; it was laden with its share of weights and obstacles. Big ones. But I had no doubts about those obstacles; they weren't insurmountable. The weights weren't unbearable. Jay and I would make it. We had what it would take. I knew it.

Ten months later came Jay's uncertainties. Against every inclination of my heart, we broke up. In the torrents of tears that followed that horrible July night, God held me. He didn't take the pain away, but like a loving parent, He kissed the wound and soothed it with His healing ointment. He tenderly bathed my wounds with His Word. He applied the salve of His promises to my torn-apart heart, and the slow healing began.

As I healed, I began to see God as I'd never seen Him before. Taking long walks with pockets full of tissues and eyes blurred with tears, I did the only thing I could—I cried out to the One who knew what I couldn't explain to anyone else. He didn't need details or background information;

He knew *everything*. The anguish of my crushed hopes, devastated dreams, and unrealized expectations reached to the deepest parts of His heart, too.

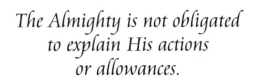

> *The Almighty is not obligated to explain His actions or allowances.*

Pain is the storm that strips away the frills of life. Life in modern America is so dressed up in all-important technology, conveniences, and luxuries that sometimes it's hard to see through to the needs of the heart. When life falls apart, though, the latest laptop doesn't bring much comfort, and a big-screen TV doesn't offer many answers.

It was in the vulnerability of this deep pain that I saw God and His sovereign sufficiency as I never had before. Every tear reminded me of my helplessness. Every suppressed sob told me I couldn't go on alone. Sifting through the scraps of my life drove me to the One who alone held the power to bring good out of the bad. I found a Friend who understood my hurt, and through pain-tinted glasses, He was even more resplendent than ever. I echoed Job's words at the end of his suffering: "My ears had heard of you but now my eyes have seen you" (Job 42:5).

Part of the mystery of suffering is God's choice to be silent in the midst of our pain. Sometimes heaven says nothing during our torrents. Cries of "why?" or "how long?" are often not answered. From atop the ash heap, Job demanded answers from God, but his tortured words seemed to bounce off the clouds. No answers came. Even at the end of the book when God finally spoke, He didn't tell Job why his life was ravaged. The Almighty is not obligated to explain His actions or allowances.

God is often silent to the questions over which we lose sleep, yet He has spoken. He has spoken through the written words of Scripture, and those words come alive when we are dying inside. The still, small voice of Scripture whispers rock-solid promises. God throws us a lifeline of the Living Word to gently pull us out of the mire and close to His heart.

In his introduction to *The Message: Job,* Eugene Peterson addresses the mystery of suffering and suggests that in the midst of suffering, Job "finds himself in an even larger mystery—the mystery of God. Perhaps the greatest mystery in suffering is how it can bring a person into the presence of God in a state of worship, full of wonder, love, and praise."[1]

Pain and a Personal Choice

Pain puts us in a vulnerable position before God, allowing us to know Him in more intimate ways. It opens the door for personal growth and character shaping. All of those are desired outcomes of my life, and I hope for your life, too. I don't like the route that's required to get there, but I wouldn't trade the results. Pain, however, doesn't automatically produce spiritual growth in my life. It's not a pill I swallow and wait for the healing to begin. Painful circumstances place me at the point of decision. I can choose to fight my way through God's plan, writhing and straining at every turn of events, or I can choose to submit to His divine direction.

Abraham stood at those points of decision pretty often

in his life, but none were as painful as the account found in
Genesis 22. The magnitude of God's command for Abraham
to sacrifice his son, Isaac, must have engulfed Abraham in
deep grief.

> *As the two of them went on together, Isaac spoke up and
> said to his father Abraham, "Father?" "Yes, my son?"
> Abraham replied. "The fire and the wood are here," Isaac
> said, "but where is the lamb for the burnt offering?"*
>
> —Genesis 22:6–7

Isaac asked his father a perfectly logical question. After
three days, the travelers were approaching their destination.
They had everything they needed for the burnt offering
except the actual object of sacrifice. The lamb was missing.
Something else is missing from the story, though. It's a
glaring omission. Go back and read the story for yourself.

> *Some time later God tested Abraham. He said to him,
> "Abraham!" "Here I am," he replied. Then God said,
> "Take your son, your only son, Isaac, whom you love,
> and go to the region of Moriah. Sacrifice him there as a
> burnt offering on one of the mountains I will tell you
> about." Early the next morning, Abraham got up and
> saddled his donkey. He took with him two of his ser-
> vants and his son Isaac. When he had cut enough wood
> for the burnt offering, he set out for the place God had
> told him about. On the third day Abraham looked up
> and saw the place in the distance. He said to his ser-
> vants, "Stay here with the donkey while I and the boy
> go over there. We will worship and then we will come
> back to you." Abraham took the wood for the burnt of-
> fering and placed it on his son Isaac, and he himself*

carried the fire and the knife. As the two of them went on together, Isaac spoke up and said to his father Abraham, "Father?" "Yes, my son?" Abraham replied. "The fire and wood are here," Isaac said, "but where is the lamb for the burnt offering?" Abraham answered, "God himself will provide the lamb for the offering, my son." And the two of them went on together. When they reached the place God had told him about, Abraham built an altar there and arranged the wood on it. He bound his son Isaac and laid him on the altar, on top of the wood. Then he reached out his hand and took the knife to slay his son. But the angel of the Lord called out to him from heaven, "Abraham! Abraham!" "Here I am," he replied. "Do not lay a hand on the boy," he said. "Do not do anything to him. Now I know that you fear God, because you have not withheld from me your son, your only son."

—Genesis 22:1–12

Did you find it? God tells Abraham to *sacrifice* his son and *early the next morning*, Abraham saddles the donkey. Three days later, father and son reach the mountain of God's choice. Abraham builds the altar, binds his son, and lifts the knife. It sounds so simple. God spoke the word, and Abraham set the alarm early.

Where is the heated argument between Sarah and Abraham about the unthinkable deed he's about to do? Where is the broken-hearted father pleading with God for the life of his son? Where is the confused man shaking his fist at God for robbing him of his greatest joy and promised heir? Where is the faithful follower finally giving in, resigned to obedience?

The story of Isaac's sacrifice is missing a struggle. Facing the most difficult test imaginable, Abraham doesn't flinch. He doesn't fight, and he doesn't try to fix it. It wasn't always this way with the Hebrews 11 hero. In fact, Abraham had a bad habit that repeatedly pokes its head into Genesis before Isaac was ever born. Abraham liked to help God when things appeared dismal.

The Fix-It Man

Not long after Abraham moved to Canaan, famine in the land made him take down his tents and head for Egypt where the grass was indeed greener. Upon arrival in the foreign country, Abraham gave Sarah her instructions.

> *I know what a beautiful woman you are. When the Egyptians see you, they will say, "This is his wife." Then they will kill me but will let you live. Say you are my sister, so that I will be treated well for your sake and my life will be spared because of you.*
>
> —Genesis 12:11–13

Understandably, Abraham was afraid for his life. He believed the men of Egypt would want his beautiful wife and kill him to get her. It appeared he was right about their desire for Sarah, because the palace officials quickly noticed her and escorted her to the palace to be Pharaoh's wife. Abraham was also right about how he would be treated as her "brother"; because of Sarah, he received sheep, cattle, donkeys, camels, and servants from Pharaoh.

I'm not so sure Abraham congratulated himself for being right. I doubt he smiled himself to sleep, alone in his tent. While his foresight and subsequent scheme had indeed saved his life, it was not without cost. In fact, the cost was enormous. He lost his wife, sacrificed her faithfulness, and forfeited his own integrity. Pharaoh paid part of the cost, too, when serious diseases descended on his house.

The story seemed to end when Pharaoh returned Sarah to Abraham and ordered them to leave the country, but it resumed years later with an almost identical chapter. This time the king's name was Abimelech, and the setting was a town called Gerar. The king summoned Sarah, Abraham's "sister," to be his wife, and not long after, Abimelech had a disconcerting dream in which God revealed the truth and consequences to him. A God-fearing man, Abimelech wasted no time correcting his mistake. God spared his life and healed the barren wombs of his entire household.

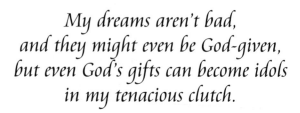

My dreams aren't bad,
and they might even be God-given,
but even God's gifts can become idols
in my tenacious clutch.

Twice in Abraham's life, he feared for his personal safety and devised his own strategy for protection. But his control of the situations created pain for all those connected.

Nowhere is this more evident than in a third instance when he devised his own strategy, the tragic story of Hagar and Ishmael. At age eighty-six, eleven years after Abraham encountered God and received the promise of a son, the nursery was still empty. I suppose we could blame Sarah for the events surrounding the birth of Ishmael. She's the one who blamed God for the absence of children in their home: "The Lord has kept me from having children." She's the one who offered the solution: "Go, sleep with my maid-servant." She's the one who assumed responsibility to see God's promise kept, "I can build a family through her" (Gen. 16:2).

But God's chosen father of His chosen nation simply agreed to do what Sarah said. He never protested on behalf of God's promises and plans, never assured his discouraged wife that God would be faithful. After eleven years, perhaps he thought God needed their help. So while God kept silent, Abraham and Sarah implemented their plan, and Hagar gave birth to Ishmael nine months later. But Abraham and Sarah had bypassed God's plan and settled for their best efforts. Once again, the lapse in faith and the inclination to fix things cost everyone dearly. The dysfunctional family was marked by jealousy, mistreatment, and hatred.

Surrender Versus Submission

Pain. Self-inflicted pain. That's what happens when God's followers settle for their own plan. That's the lesson Abraham learned before God ever asked him to sacrifice Isaac. At an earlier point in his life, he might have tried to work an alternative, but when God laid the test of all time in front of him, Abraham didn't flinch.

Instead, he waived his right to his son. Abraham didn't surrender; he submitted. Don't miss the difference. Surrender only happens after a struggle, a fight to maintain control. Abraham had already struggled in his life, clinging desperately to dreams he thought would never become reality, and he had learned the hard way that his hands in God's plan only created more hardship. Abraham was past surrendering. There was no fight, no attempt to intervene on God's behalf. He just followed. God said the word, and Abraham obeyed.

Sometimes I look down and realize my hands are clutching dreams—dreams of my Prince Charming in our suburban castle, surrounded by a white picket fence, and guarded by a floppy-eared barking ferocity. My dreams aren't bad, and they might even be God-given, but even God's gifts can become idols in my tenacious clutch. They become all-consuming elements of my life, and they don't even exist! If God hasn't transformed my dreams into reality, I sometimes assume the responsibility to help Him.

Remember the Rubik's Cube? In grade school, the multicolored block puzzle entertained my classmates and me for many recess hours. It was a monumental achievement for me to get just one side of the cube completed. Then I'd look at the other five sides and realize how woefully inadequate I was to put the whole puzzle together. No matter how I twisted and turned things, it only got worse. In my hands, the original design would never be restored.

With a lot of patience on my part and an expert series of twists on His part, life takes on a whole new dimension.

I had a classmate who was a master with the cube, and in frustration, I'd finally hand the mess over to him. The first thing he always did was destroy the part I'd worked so hard to assemble. He'd twist and turn my one-sided masterpiece, until it looked just like the disaster *I* could make.

It was once again seemingly scrambled beyond repair. Inevitably, though, with a little bit of patience and a lot of wrenching turns, his thorough knowledge of the puzzle always prevailed. With order restored, the cube became a perfect design of color and symmetry.

I always knew it *could* come together, but try as I might, it would never happen in my hands. Left to me, it was limited to a one-sided solution at best. But in the hands of a master, the scrambled, twisted mess wasn't even a challenge.

In the struggle to retain my life dreams and somehow make them happen, I've sometimes felt like a Rubik's Cube. Just when I get one side of my life falling into place and making some sense, I realize that so much else is beyond my control. I am helpless to solve things, and in fact, I make a bigger mess and create more pain.

It's only when I hand it back to the Master Puzzler that there is hope. He may twist and change the whole puzzle, and it may appear to me that He's just created another disaster beyond repair, yet I know that my puzzle is never out of His control. Sometimes the transitions, twists, and turns of life make me creak and groan. I don't understand, and I don't see the solution. Sometimes I wonder what on earth He is doing with my life, but I'm so thankful that He understands what I can't. With a lot of patience on my part and an expert series of twists on His part, life takes on a whole new dimension.

The Master Puzzler often takes His time revealing that new dimension. He may choose to turn the cube a little more slowly, drawing out the groan of the jumbled mess. He may allow great pain to course through my life. But He knows the solution; He knows the way I must take. And He can get me there.

By the way, I don't even try to work Rubik's Cubes

anymore—even one side. I guess after enough frustrating bouts with the puzzle, I learned to leave it to those who know what they are doing. Abraham learned to do the same. After enough frustrating endeavors, he left his life in the hands of the One who knew what He was doing. Abraham knew God wouldn't disappoint him. Better yet, He surprised him.

Noah: Living with Perseverance

I'm afraid that if he doesn't come back, that it'll hurt so much that I'll shrivel up and I'll never be able to love anyone ever again.

—Kate, *French Kiss*

*S*am Baldwin loses his young wife to cancer in the 1993 Hollywood romantic comedy *Sleepless in Seattle*. In the wake of her death, Sam packs up his son, Jonah, and moves across the country to Seattle, Washington, to escape memories lurking around every Chicago corner. He quickly discovers that a fresh start doesn't lessen the pain, and plodding through daily routines in her absence is still excruciating. Sometimes the pain is even paralyzing. Late one night, a desperate eight-year-old Jonah dials a midnight talk show host, seeking advice to ease his dad's pain. At Dr. Marsha Field-Stone's request, an unwilling Sam takes the phone and is asked by the psychologist what he plans to do about his grief. With a heavy sigh, Sam replies, "Well, Dr. Marsha, I'm going to get out of bed every morning and breathe in and out all day long, and then after a while I won't have to remind myself to get out of bed in the morning and breathe in and out. And then after a while I won't think about how I had it great and perfect for a while."

I don't know about you, but I recognize this feeling. There have been bone-chilling winters in my life when God has allowed stormy squalls of pain to rage around me. On the accompanying dark, icy mornings, I've awakened wishing I could just roll over again to escape the agony. I've pulled my tired toes to the floor, put one foot in front of the other, and reluctantly inched into another day no brighter than the one before. Breathe in. Breathe out. The crushing pain of a shattered heart is intense, but life manages to go on whether or not I think *I* can. Somehow the days become weeks, the calendar pictures keep changing, and I make it through.

What Is Perseverance?

Hebrews 12:1 assures me that God has marked out my race, no matter what sort of pain or pleasure it includes. Reality affirms that my race, and yours too, often includes suffering. Notice, though, how God wisely prefaced the assurance of His sovereignty: "Let us run with *perseverance* the race marked out for us" (emphasis mine). He's in control of the course, but I am the one who has to persevere through its twists and turns.

Perseverance follows in the footprints of pain. When the storm clouds thicken, perseverance closes the shutters and gathers provisions. When the wind rips branches off surrounding trees, perseverance takes cover in the basement. When the house breaks into pieces like collapsing tooth-picks, perseverance thumbs through the Yellow Pages for another builder. When the storm has passed, perseverance weathers what's left.

Perseverance is pressing on with determination through dismal days because I know God is good and I believe His promises are true.

When used in Scripture, the word *perseverance* implies the carrying of a heavy load, like a camel crossing the desert. It means to stay under a burden and not collapse. It means I plod across life's arid plains with weights on my back, but somehow, instead of falling in a heap, I actually gain strength from the whole process.

Perseverance is not just hanging on with clenched fists until the tough times pass. Instead, it's hanging on with a dogged trust in the One who allows the tough times. It's pressing on with determination through dismal days be-cause I know God is good and I believe His promises are true. When I don't perceive the good or see the direct ful-fillment of His promises, faith steps up. Faith is being so sure of what I hope for and so certain of what I do not see that I can keep going. I can have an endurance rooted in hope, a tenacity driven by the perspective of God at work in my life.

Perseverance is me "re-rewriting" this chapter, convinced I have something to say if the words will just come together.

Perseverance is bride-to-have-been-Laura altering a never-worn bridesmaid's dress for a friend who stayed with her on her canceled wedding weekend. Perseverance is my friend Kathy talking about how God has helped her cope with the sudden death of her two teen-aged sons. Perseverance is Jesus dragging a heavy cross on His shredded shoulders, seeing a very desperate you and a really pathetic me in the distance.

Wanting the Bottom Line

This kind of endurance would be so much easier, I think, if God would give me a glimpse of what's ahead. If He would just answer a few questions for me, I'm sure I could press on with more enthusiasm. I'd like Him to disclose the bottom line on some of the uncertainties of my life, because I know it would help me press toward the finish line.

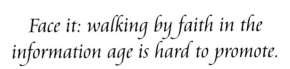

Face it: walking by faith in the information age is hard to promote.

In fact, God and I could avoid some of my spiritual temper tantrums if He would just speak up. A spiritual temper tantrum is the internal fury of *knowing* God is good, loving, and kind, but kicking and screaming about the way He chooses to show it. It's knowing that His will is perfect and that only following His way can bring peace, happiness, and fulfillment; but at the same time, feeling that He certainly could have accomplished His will in a less painful way. It's wondering why *this* lesson had to be learned *this* way. In short, it's not understanding why God does what He does.

Face it: walking by faith in the information age is hard to promote. When the world's drivers are speeding down the information superhighway, it's tough to walk by faith on the side of the road.

I just think it would be easier to know.

Then again, maybe not.

Along with millions of other Americans, I elbowed my way into a swarming theater to see the 1997 blockbuster movie *Titanic*. The retelling of the fate of the "unsinkable" ship topped the charts for sixteen weeks.

A ship that was built by experts and commanded by veterans plunged to the ocean floor on the calm, starry night of April 14, 1912, extinguishing the lives of fifteen hundred stunned passengers. It didn't sink because of human error but because of human arrogance. Warnings were ignored, preparation for disaster was insufficient, and the unthinkable happened.

Cinematically speaking, it was a great movie; emotionally, it was horrible. For 197 minutes, a knot grew in my stomach because I knew the awful truth. I knew what the 2200 passengers didn't know. They were doomed; the boat was going to sink. Over half of them were going to freeze to death in the icy grip of the North Atlantic Ocean. All of their elegance and extravagance would be shrouded in the rusty rubbish of the sunken ship.

As I watched, I hoped against futile hope that somehow the iceberg would be avoided, the boat would be repaired, miraculous lifeboats would fall from the sky, the lost would be rescued. I hoped, but I also knew, it wouldn't be. It couldn't be. The story had already been written. Fates had been determined. History dictated the ending, and even Hollywood couldn't change it.

The whole experience made me think of Noah, not because of the boat or the water, and not even because of the shared fate of so many people. I thought of Noah because *he knew*. From the very start when God said "build an ark" to the horrible finish after God shut the door, Noah watched the horror unfold. He knew the story; God told him exactly what was going to happen. "I am going to put an end to all people, for the earth is filled with violence because of them. I am surely going to destroy both them and the earth" (Gen. 6:13).

Noah and Knowing

I've often pictured Noah as a long-bearded, shriveled, old man, hammering away on his boat while his neighbors laughed. Really, though, the Flood narrative in Genesis is silent on the events of the construction years. In chapter six, God gave Noah a command and a set of explicit directions, and Scripture records that Noah followed God's words.

We can't be sure what else took place during those years, perhaps as many as one hundred. We can safely assume Noah was busy. We can probably assume that his neighbors were mystified and perhaps amused by his activities. He was, after all, building a large sailing vessel in a place where there was nowhere to launch it. But even the best joke gets old, and I bet after a couple years, the novelty wore off. He was just a fanatic, the local loon, not worth much of their attention. So maybe they laughed at him, perhaps they scorned the God who issued the order, but I doubt they tortured him for a hundred years. He just built.

Building a boat as tall as a five-story building and longer than a football field was an overwhelming task. Year after painful year, though, Noah persevered with an even heavier weight—the knowledge that his neighbors were going to perish. The people who lived next door, those he had known for hundreds of years, would be destroyed. Scripture records that Noah preached to the people, but we also know that no one paid much attention. No one really seemed to care about his words or his work.

Perseverance is not glamorous or attention getting. In fact, it can be pretty lonely. After a while, we stop noticing people who persevere. No credit to us, we tend to forget, and they become part of the scenery, part of the routine of life. They trudge through life's lonely trenches carrying pain we can't even imagine. When nobody notices, when nobody appreciates the pain, perseverance causes them to press on.

Noah was familiar with those lonely trenches; he was surrounded by armies of people going the other direction, masses of humanity blindly headed for destruction. I've always admired his example of perseverance, simply because he pressed on when no one seemingly understood or cared what he was doing. I appreciate the depth of his faith even more, though, after seeing the movie *Titanic*. Noah pressed on with a full understanding of what was to come. God entrusted him with the horrible bottom line, removing all hope for a happy ending.

Noah deserves the perseverance prize of the ages for his actions. He pressed on through the horror of imminent disaster because, by faith, he anchored his life and heart in the One who knew best.

If Noah could persevere with full knowledge of the story's end, I can surely follow his example and persevere along a much easier route of *not* knowing the bottom line.

By faith Noah, when warned about things not yet seen, in holy fear built an ark to save his family. By his faith he condemned the world and became heir of the righteousness that comes by faith.

—Hebrews 11:7

Pressing On in Obedience

Noah's perseverance was, first of all, driven by obedience. *In holy fear he built an ark.* When God issued a command, Noah obeyed it. It was as simple as that. Repeatedly in the Genesis story, he is said to have done everything just as the Lord commanded him. Noah was a devout man who obeyed divine instructions.

Tasha, my family's last dog, obeyed instructions, too, but not without the restraint of a leash. She was a sweet dog with huge, milky-brown eyes, but she was also a spunky dog with a stubborn mind of her own. Prior to several sessions at obedience school, she was sheer frustration to walk around the driveway, much less around the neighborhood. She tugged on her choker collar until she hacked instead of panted; she bounced back and forth in front of my feet; she pranced, yanked, and reared up on the leash. Even after obedience school, Tasha still required a leash and a pronged collar. That dog could never walk at my side without some sort of restraint. Her eventual obedience was motivated by jabs in her neck. Tasha complied because it hurt if she didn't.

Noah walked with God; he wasn't walked by God.

Noah didn't obey because God tugged on his leash. The obedience of Noah went beyond doing what God said simply because the results of *not* doing so would be painful. Genesis 6:9 reveals that Noah "walked with God." He lived his life circumspectly, carefully walking a path that lined up with God's footsteps. He didn't run ahead with his own plan, or trail behind reluctant to follow, or tug stubbornly in the opposite direction. Noah walked *with* God; he wasn't walked *by* God. His obedience grew out of a relationship, a friendship. They walked side by side, and Noah trusted the heart of his heavenly Friend. It was a trust that enabled him to persevere in spite of the impending disaster.

Pressing On for the Practical

In addition to obedience, Noah's perseverance was also driven by something very practical. Noah built the ark to save his family. When God passed along the blueprints for the boat, He also gave Noah the roster for the ark's inhabitants. Two by two the animals would come, and Noah, his wife, his sons, and his sons' wives would join them. Only eight human beings would be admitted into the ark and saved from the Flood.

On a grand, noble scale, Noah built the boat to save humanity and the creatures of the world, but sometimes grand, noble reasons are too big for small, ordinary people. In His grace and understanding of the human race, God gave Noah a more personal motivation to persevere. His wife. His sons. His future. Noah built the ark to rescue the ones he loved from destruction. If the temptation ever came to quit (and it probably did), if ever Noah lost sight of the goal, all he had to do was go home for lunch. The faces of his family drove him back outside, hammer in hand, with renewed energy to tackle the mountain of lumber on his front lawn.

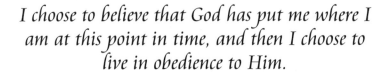

I choose to believe that God has put me where I am at this point in time, and then I choose to live in obedience to Him.

I'm no Noah (and neither are you). In fact, compared to Noah and his floating zoo, my job measures pretty small on the scale of global impact. My struggles, even if they drag on for months and years, pale beside the difficulties of Noah, who quite possibly endured a century of adversity. It's hard to compete.

Fortunately, as far as God is concerned, I don't have to compete. He's given me my own set of struggles and adversities, and then He points me to an example like Noah to learn the way through.

The struggles of singleness are real, and they are significant. Being single in a world designed by God for partnership brings pain. I fight the feelings of "unsettledness," tempted to wonder if and when marriage will come. I cradle tiny babies in my arms, filled with wistful longings to have my own. I go solo to social events populated by couples and feel the all-too-familiar stabs of aloneness. I get weary of waking up to the furry face of Edward, my stuffed elephant. I tire of digging up dates to attend friends' weddings. I battle the loneliness of not having a constant, committed companion.

Trudging through the trenches of singleness takes perseverance. Sometimes it's perseverance generated by sheer obedience—a gritted-teeth act of submission. I *choose* to believe that God has put me where I am at this point in time, and then I *choose* to live in obedience to Him. Like Noah, though, I'm not content to be yanked into line by the disciplinary hand of God. I'd rather hold that hand and walk in trust next to my Friend. I want to press on because I'm so in step with the Creator of the universe that walking a difficult road is an opportunity to sidle a little closer to Him, to hold His hand a little tighter.

God knows, however, that regardless of how much I want to walk with Him, there will be stretches of road when I'll loosen my grip on His hand. My walk with God will be more like a stumble or a flat-on-my-face fall. In those places on the journey, I'll tug on the leash and strain to have things my way, or I'll just sit down and stubbornly refuse to move.

It's in those times that I need to take a step back. I need to go home for lunch. I need to remind myself of some really practical reasons why God might have routed the course this way. I'm not pretending to know the reasons why I'm still single, but I do know that even in the hardest of situations, God often gives tiny glimpses into some good things He's doing. Backing away and forcing myself to see the positive helps me press on. Some people call it the cloud's silver lining or the rose in the thorns. I think it's a whole lot more. I like to call it walking on the water.

Walking on the Water

In the darkest hours of a first-century night, twelve tired men struggled against the relentless waves of the Sea of Galilee. Water splashed over the sides of their battered fishing boat and sloshed around their ankles while they strained at the oars. They hung on and hoped to outlast the storm. Just when they thought the situation couldn't get any worse, it did. They looked up and saw it . . . either they were going to die in the storm, or they were going to be killed by the approaching ghost.

Give them a little credit. It had been a *really* long day, colored every shade of the emotional spectrum, and it wasn't over yet. Beginning with the bad news of John the Baptist's death, the day continued with throngs of thousands demanding attention, and it ended with an all-you-can-eat feast from a sack lunch. The disciples were undoubtedly exhausted, and then the storm hit in the middle of the lake. It's no wonder they thought they saw a ghost. Jesus' words, "It is I. Don't be afraid," awakened them from their nightmare, quelled their terror, and gave them cause to think they might make it through the storm after all.

It took a little faith and a lot of guts for Peter to step out, but I guarantee he never regretted it.

But making it through the storm wasn't enough for Peter. He wasn't content to hang on to the sides of the boat, praying for the waves to die down. He didn't want to bail like crazy to keep the boat from sinking; there were eleven other guys doing that stuff. No, not Peter. "Lord, if it's you, . . . tell me to come to you on the water" (Matt. 14:28). Peter wanted to walk on the very waves that blasted against his boat.

The stormy waters became his platform to get closer to Jesus. They paved the way for an unbelievable experience, an incredible walk of faith that catapulted Peter into uncharted waters. It's amazing to me that none of Peter's friends hopped out of the boat to join his strides. Maybe their heads were buried too deeply between their knees, or maybe they didn't think it would work for them, or maybe they just weren't willing to loosen their whitened knuckles from their familiar grip on the boat.

I don't know why they stayed put, but I do know what they missed. The blessing. The thrill. The miraculous. It took a little faith and a lot of guts for Peter to step out, but I guarantee he never regretted it. Peter took a hike on the same water his buddies were bailing out of the boat.

Singleness can be a platform, water to walk on instead of a storm to wait out. Without family responsibilities, I am free to pour my energies into local church ministries. With just me and my paycheck, I can sometimes afford to encourage friends with impulsive gifts. Without the encumbrances of someone else's schedule, I can give extra attention to developing reading, writing, and study habits.

I don't know what positive results of singleness you might find in your own life, but I do know they are there if you will look. Maybe your pain paves a footpath into somebody's heart; you can understand them like you never could before. Perhaps you are better able to focus your energies on your relationship with God. Your loneliness might send you running to the arms of the ever-present Source of love. Learning to walk on the water transforms the storm into an adventure, an opportunity. It takes a little more work and definitely more faith; it's much easier to sit in the boat until the storm blows over. Storms usually do. But while you're sitting, you're also missing the best parts of the trip.

One Page at a Time

I don't know what's ahead for me in life. I don't know what other storms are gathering in the distance, but frankly,

I don't want to know anymore. That would be like knowing the end of a book. Foreknowledge ruins the rest of the chapters because it eliminates my participation in the story line. There's no wondering about the outcome, no enjoyment of figuring things out, no thrill at the slow revelation of clues. Not knowing the ending allows me to enjoy every page, trusting the author to be in total charge of the story. I can savor every twist of the unraveling plot.

One of my favorite twentieth-century characters is Corrie ten Boom. She and her family housed and cared for Jews during Hitler's Holocaust. In her book, *The Hiding Place*, the endearing Dutch woman tells a tale from a childhood trip on the train with her father.

> I asked Father about a poem we had read at school the winter before. One line had described "a young man whose face was not shadowed by sexsin." I had been far to shy to ask the teacher what it meant, and Mama had blushed scarlet when I consulted her. In those days just after the turn of the century sex was never discussed, even at home.
>
> So the line had stuck in my head. "Sex," I was pretty sure, meant whether you were a boy or a girl, and "sin" made Tante Jans very angry, but what the two together meant I could not imagine. And so, seated next to Father in the train compartment, I suddenly asked, "Father, what is sexsin?"
>
> He turned to look at me, as he always did when answering a question, but to my surprise he said nothing. At last he stood up, lifted his traveling case from the rack over our heads, and set it on the floor.

"Will you carry it off the train, Corrie?" he said.

I stood up and tugged at it. It was crammed with the watches and spare parts he had purchased that morning.

"It's too heavy," I said.

"Yes," he said. "And it would be a pretty poor father who would ask his little girl to carry such a load. It's the same way, Corrie, with knowledge. Some knowledge is too heavy for children. When you are older and stronger, you can bear it. For now you must trust me to carry it for you."[1]

Some knowledge is too heavy for children. I'm glad I have a Father to carry it for me, and I'm glad He's got another hand to hold.

5

Moses: Living Through Rejection

*I think it's me, I do, because he used to look at me and
I used to see myself in his eyes. . . . And then, things
started to change, and the harder I tried to be what he
wanted me to be, the less I saw myself in his eyes. I just,
one day I looked, and I was gone.*

—Birdee Pruitt, *Hope Floats*

*M*iss Widder, do you know you have a *big* zit on your
face? Right . . . there!"

I was so glad Sally pointed this out to me. She apparently thought that during my mirror exercises that morning, I hadn't noticed there was a zit the size of Mount
Kilimanjaro on my cheek. (Unfortunately, it wasn't nearly
so beautiful.)

Frankly, Sally drove me crazy. For every round of recess
duty that year, I had a shadow—except I've never tripped

over my two-dimensional shadow or been insulted by it. Sally didn't seem to realize that recess is supposed to be a break for the teacher, too. I think she thought I'd get lonely if she didn't hover near me, pointing out facial flaws or asking personal questions like "Why don't you have a boyfriend?" (I *am* surprised she never claimed the two things were related.)

As exasperating as Sally was to me, I had a hard time being angry with her. I knew why she stayed so close. It wasn't to keep *me* company; it was to keep *her* company. Sally didn't have many friends. If she had wanted to play the team game on the playground that day, she would've been the last one picked. If she had wanted to swing on the monkey bars like her nimble classmates, she wouldn't have gotten far off the ground. If she had wanted to run races or skip rope or play foursquare, she probably would've twisted her ankle in her higher-heeled shoes.

For singles like me in the post-college years, singleness is a state of constant rejection.

She always said she didn't want to do all those other things, and maybe she was telling the truth, but I think she stuck by me because it was safer. While I didn't exactly embrace her, she knew I wouldn't reject her either.

The Results of Rejection

We've all felt the pain of rejection in some arena of life. We've groped around at the bottom of the barrel, wondering how we'll ever climb the ladder back into the light of day. Each barrel is marked with its own label—"Didn't Make the Team," or "Lost a Best Friend," or "Failed Geometry," or "Divorced Parents," or "Broken Relationships."

One of the barrels in my life is marked "Singleness," and I've spent my fair share of time at the bottom of it, as have many other single adults. For singles like me in the post-college years, singleness is a state of constant rejection. Nobody has chosen to marry me yet, while all around me it seems that everybody else is being paired off. The fact is that I've been rejected, even if it's been by guys I *didn't* want to marry; the point is, most of them didn't want to marry me either. Sometimes, though, being single has meant being rejected by someone I *did* want to marry. In any form, rejection is extremely painful.

While the labels on the barrels may be varied, the resulting pains are similar. Loneliness—nobody understands me and nobody wants to be with me; I am alone. Inadequacy—there must be something wrong with me and that's why this happened. Fear—I don't want to try anymore because I might get hurt again.

Rejection grips the human heart with its powerful tentacles of loneliness, inadequacy, and fear.

The pain is deep, and the effects can be far-reaching, but rejection doesn't have to be fatal. There *is* a way out of the barrel, whatever the label. Moses was a man who had reserved seating in the bottom of his barrel. Yet God used that rejection to shape his life and prepare him for a great work.

From the Top of the Mountain to the Bottom of the Barrel

A Hebrew male born during the reign of a ruthless Pharaoh, Moses should have been killed at birth. Instead, in disobedience to the king's command, his mother hid him for three months and then set him sailing in a basket on the Nile River. Pulled from the water by Pharaoh's daughter, Moses grew up with the luxuries of royalty instead of the stigma of slavery.

When he grew up, Moses turned his back on royal privilege and title, choosing instead to identify with his people. One day he went to watch the Hebrew slaves at work. As he watched, Moses was enraged at the way his people were treated. Stepping to the defense of a slave, hoping to somehow make a difference, Moses looked both ways and crossed the line; he killed an Egyptian and then hid the body in the sand, confident no one had seen him.

The very next day, Moses returned to the work site, and this time he encountered two Hebrews fighting. When he asked one of them why he was hitting the other, Moses got an answer he did not expect: "Who made you ruler and judge over us? Are you thinking of killing me as you killed the Egyptian?" (Exod. 2:14).

Out of terror, Moses ran like a rabbit to the desert of Midian. Moses, the man who had been "educated in all the wisdom of the Egyptians" counted heads of smelly sheep in a blazing desert for the next forty years. He was far away from the threat of capture, but he was even farther away from what he thought God had called him to do—help his people.

Moses was alone. He'd left the palace, his picture was in the post office, and his own people had rejected him. Moses had assumed the Israelites would realize that God was using him to rescue them, but they did not. They didn't embrace his efforts on their behalf or appreciate his identification with them. Instead they spat words of hostility in his face. They told him they didn't need or want his help.

Forty years is a long time to ponder failures and live in the shadow of rejection. (Talk about self-esteem problems!) Yet even in that time, God was working in the heart of a confused, crushed but precious shepherd, preparing Moses to lead His people out of Egypt and to the Promised Land. At the end of those forty years, God appeared to Moses in a burning bush and called him to return to Egypt as His chosen deliverer. Moses balked. He did more than balk; he nearly bolted. Offering more excuses than a tardy student, Moses did his best to get out of the job.

> *Who am I, that I should go to Pharaoh and bring the Israelites out of Egypt?*
>
> —Exodus 3:11

> *Suppose I go to the Israelites and say to them, "The God of your fathers has sent me to you," and they ask me, "What is his name?" Then what shall I tell them?*
>
> —Exodus 3:13

> *What if they do not believe me or listen to me and say, "The Lord did not appear to you"?*
>
> —Exodus 4:1

O Lord, I have never been eloquent, neither in the past nor since you have spoken to your servant. I am slow of speech and tongue.

—Exodus 4:10

O Lord, please send someone else to do it.

—Exodus 4:13

Moses was milksop, a cowering man with no confidence, ambition, or willingness. He was paralyzed. That's what rejection does. It grips the human heart with its powerful tentacles of loneliness, inadequacy, and fear. It squeezes nearly any sense of value out of the human soul.

If you've ever been caught in the clutch of rejection, you know how hard it is to pry open the grip. In fact, it's a job only God can do, and that's where the rest of the story of Moses gives great comfort. From the flaming foliage, God spoke healing to Moses, gently uncoiling the tentacles of rejection from around the heart of His chosen leader. That encounter with the Living God released Moses from the bondage of a battered self-concept and freed him to fulfill the great work God had for him.

Loneliness—Wanting an "It"

I've said good-bye to more friends over the years than I care to count, and it never gets any easier. Fortunately in a world of telephones, postage stamps, and e-mail, it's not impossible to maintain relationships, even at great distances. If I want, I can always hop a plane or fill my gas tank for a weekend of catching up.

But it's not the same as having an "it," a group nearby where I always belong and am always wanted. My best friend from college and I invented this term one night when we were by ourselves in a dorm room. It was a night when everyone else had gone to a local amusement park, and for an unknown reason, no one had invited us. We looked at each other and wondered why we had been excluded from the group, why we'd been eliminated from the "it."

Having an "it" is very important to a single person. I once heard a pastor describe marriage as the "breaking away and gluing together" of two people. First they each break away from their own families, and then they are glued to each other. For adult singles, we've done the breaking away, and there's no one to be glued to. We are stuck instead by ourselves in an in-between phase we never planned on, an in-between phase that was never part of God's original design, either.

Loneliness comes easily when you're not glued to somebody. One of the greatest longings of the human heart is to be deeply loved by another human being, to live side by side with someone who carries you in his or her heart, to be a lifelong part of somebody else. Being single means I don't have a permanent "it," that one special person who is committed to caring about the details of my life. There's no one who knows me intimately and *still* likes me; there's no one who has chosen to stick by me no matter what. It leaves me with a sense of incompleteness and aloneness.

Moses may not have dealt with the absence of a life-long "it," but he was certainly in a lonely position. As a rejected son of Egypt and a rejected Israelite, he was cut off from forty years of life. Forty years of relationships. Every person he'd ever known in his life was gone, and as a fugitive, he probably didn't have too many opportunities to connect with those he left behind.

While in Midian, Moses married Zipporah and began his family. He started a new life, but it's not so easy to forget the past. The name he chose for his son indicates that Moses hadn't forgotten who he was and what he'd become; he named him Gershom, saying, "I have become an alien in a foreign land" (Exod. 2:22). Those are lonely words.

Lonely or Alone?

After forty years of being an alien, Moses met God in a bush and heard His words of comfort. They were words of comfort to a lonely man being called to do a lonely job. Moses would lead the suffering slaves out of bondage and through the wilderness. God knew the loneliness Moses had already experienced after being rejected by his own people. He also knew the lonely days ahead for Moses, who would be rejected repeatedly by the same people as he assumed the role of deliverer. Leadership can be extremely lonely, and God offered the only antidote for loneliness when He told Moses, "I will be with you" (Exod. 3:12).

Loneliness is a condition for which I must find a remedy. Aloneness is just the state of being by myself.

Like Moses, I am never alone, regardless of how I may feel. I have a friend who argues this point with me, protesting, "But I can't see God." She's right about that, but she's wrong to think that not seeing God somehow limits the comfort He can bring. The comfort comes when I *choose* to see Him. Evidence of His presence surrounds me, even in the hardest of times. I am lonely when I ignore it. I am lonely when I close my eyes to His presence, shutting out the One who is always there.

There's a difference between being lonely and being alone. Loneliness is a condition for which I must find a remedy. Aloneness is just the state of being by myself. It's the very definition of singleness. Often aloneness causes loneliness, but it doesn't have to. Elizabeth Yates puts aloneness into perspective with her words in *Up the Golden Stair*.

> Sometime or another each one of us will face aloneness. It was only when I did that I began to learn the real meaning of the word. . . . It does not matter how rich and rare and satisfying the relationships we have known have been . . . there comes a time when each one must see himself or herself as an integer in the Universe: not dependant on or conjoined with anyone else. Something begins to happen then. The only way I know how to say it is that we become aware as never before of our relationship with God, and the actual definition of the word alone—All plus one—has personal meaning.
>
> When this began to work itself through me, I was acutely conscious of the one; only gradually could I accept the All. But, in time, it became like a great protective mountain rising behind me.[1]

All of Him plus one of me. That's a permanent "it." But while He's always there being my "it," I'm not always so faithful to Him. It requires great mental discipline to fight loneliness. It takes constant effort to walk closely with Him, drawing upon His companionship. It takes work to practice

His presence. But sticking close to my "It" is the only thing that gets me through the lonely times. In fact, God invites me to do more than "get through" lonely times; He invites me to know Him in deeper ways, ways impossible without the pain of rejection. Only when the "land of loneliness [becomes] the land of hunger for God . . . of belonging to God and understanding that God alone matters" can I hope to make it.[2]

Inadequacy—Looking Over Your Shoulder

God loosened the grip of Moses's loneliness by promising His presence, but He also pried the tentacle of inadequacy from around Moses's bruised heart. The excuses of Moses mirror just how deeply those feelings went.

"Who am I, that I should go to Pharaoh and bring the Israelites out of Egypt?"

Once upon an Egyptian lifetime, Moses was sure that God wanted to use him to help the Hebrew slaves. I bet he marveled at the way God pieced his life together to prepare him for the job. Being born a Hebrew, but being reared in the palace gave him connections with both worlds. It made him the ideal candidate to negotiate terms between Israelites and Egyptians.

"I am slow of speech and tongue."

I'd feel sorry for a stuttering Moses, called to be the spokesman of a nation. The truth is, though, that he wasn't a stammering, dull-witted communicator. In fact, according to Stephen's speech to the Sanhedrin in Acts 7:22, Moses was "powerful in speech and action." He knew how to hold a crowd and make things happen.

What happened to the man hand-picked and God-equipped to be a leader? That's an easy answer; he ran at lightning speed into the wall of rejection. Everything he thought he understood about his purpose and direction in life evaporated into arid skies. Dreams and plans for the future dried up when his own countrymen, the very people he thought he was called to lead, rejected him.

When Moses took off his shoes on that holy ground, I think he looked over his shoulder, too. Confused about his own calling and uncertain about his abilities, he was sure God must be talking to someone else. Obviously, he'd mis-read God's plan about his leadership once before, and he wasn't about to do it again. That "misreading" landed him in the desert for forty years. (Little did he know that this second interaction would land him in the desert for forty more years—with a mass of grumbling people instead of a flock of bleating sheep!) Moses wasn't about to make the same mistake twice.

Rejection had eaten away at his self-esteem. It damaged his vision of God's calling, and it destroyed his confidence in his God-given abilities and strengths. It raised constant questions about his value and significance.

Another Kind of Passover

Like Moses, I have watched God shape some puzzle pieces of my life over the years, and I've marveled at the way He seems to be working the puzzle. I've shaken my head at how perfect things seemed, how wonderfully He planned the picture. But like Moses, I've also landed in a desert, wondering if I saw His picture all wrong. I can relate to his feelings of inadequacy, because I, too, have experienced rejection that's shaken the core of who I am.

There *is* a certain sense of inadequacy that grows out of being repeatedly "passed over" by single guys, but while I ask myself why and wonder what's wrong with me, those questions aren't core-shaking. It's when I've invested myself in a significant dating relationship only to have it break apart that the darkest clouds of inadequacy gather and shroud the horizon in blackness. Long-held dreams and deep desires spill out of a broken heart, leaving a lifeless mass of confusion, insecurity, and the inescapable fear that they are gone forever.

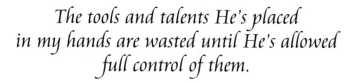

The tools and talents He's placed in my hands are wasted until He's allowed full control of them.

When I've given the very best of who I am, when I've shared my innermost thoughts and fears, when I've trusted totally and unreservedly and *then* am rejected, there's a devastating loss of confidence. To be in a relationship where unconditional love is proclaimed and promised, and then revoked, is one of the greatest losses the human heart can sustain. The message that travels from a broken heart to a logical brain says "Your best wasn't good enough. You are inadequate and incapable of having the kind of relationship God designed for men and women."

Thankfully, God didn't let Moses get away with his excuses, and His answer to the timid shepherd also addresses the "logical conclusions" reached by little brains. "Who gave man his mouth? Who makes him deaf or mute? Who gives him sight or makes him blind? Is it not I, the LORD? Now go; *I will help you speak and will teach you what to say*" (Exod. 4:11–12, emphasis mine).

Moses *was* inadequate, and so are the rest of us. That's precisely the point. God gave Moses an object lesson to make His message perfectly clear. He told him to take the staff in his hand and throw it on the ground. He did, and it turned into a snake. God told him to pick it up. He did, and it turned into a staff. God told Moses that the transformation of the staff and snake would convince the Israelites that Moses, the man they'd once rejected, was their chosen leader. It's as if God was saying to Moses, "I'm responsible for what happens through your life, not you. You just obey me, and I'll take care of the results."

God takes what we have (more accurately, what He's given us!), and He provides the power. The tools and talents He's placed in my hands *are* wasted until He's allowed full control of them. Then, and only then, through Him I can do exactly what He has in mind for me to do. He is sufficient, and He's the one controlling what happens.

Fear—Running from Opportunity

Moses's final desperate attempt at getting away from God's calling is found in Exodus 4:13, "O Lord, please send someone else to do it." In spite of all God's assurances and promises, Moses couldn't find the courage to tackle the task. He just didn't want to do it. Moses was caught in rejection's grip of fear. He didn't want to take the risk, didn't want to face the hurt, didn't want to pay the price.

At this point in the burning bush story, God gets angry. Four times He had offered Moses the promises and power necessary for him to face the opposition and accomplish the job. Even after all of that, though, Moses was still stuck. "I can't do it," he seems to say. "I just can't do it."

God's angry answer to Moses should've been "Do it anyway! I have chosen you, and you *are* the man for the job. Quit your griping and get packing." Moses should've been scared into accepting the job, if nothing else, but look at what happened instead.

> *What about your brother, Aaron the Levite? I know he can speak well. He is already on his way to meet you, and his heart will be glad when he sees you. You shall speak to him and put words in his mouth; I will help both of you speak and will teach you what to do. He will speak to the people for you, and it will be as if he were your mouth and as if you were God to him. But take this staff in your hand so you can perform miraculous signs with it.*
>
> —Exodus 4:14–17

God didn't lambaste Moses back to Egypt. Instead, He gave him Aaron, a tangible reminder of His comfort. He provided a partner to walk the tough road ahead, offering a steady source of support.

Modern-Day Manna

God understands humanity. He knows that we are so very weak, in spite of our best efforts to be strong. God has showered us with promises that ought to be enough to send us anywhere, to do any job. But the truth is, we don't. We freeze in fear. Thankfully, God in His mercy doesn't zap us for our timid resistance. Instead, in His compassion, He dispenses grace beyond what we even thought to ask.

There's manna for the moment.
And there will be manna for
tomorrow's moments, too.

God's grace is like manna. You remember the small loaves of bread God supplied for the Israelites morning after desert morning. Do you remember how He supplied it? Just what they needed, just for the day. God didn't let them stockpile manna in the pantry. Every morning, the wanderers awoke to little loaves outside their tents. If they tried to store it up, it rotted. If they didn't bother to gather any, they went hungry.

God always provides the sustenance to press on through the wilderness. Somehow, in my wilderness experiences, He manages to give grace that lets me take another step. If I look at the miles stretching across the sand, I am engulfed in fear. There *is* no way I can make it. But if I look at the loaf in front of my foot, I can take the next step. There's manna for the moment. And there will be manna for tomorrow's moments, too. When I get there, He'll provide.

Singles often wander in the wilderness of broken relationships, with fear as their companion. Having been deeply wounded by the rejection of someone they loved, they greatly fear future relationships. It's hard to even think about getting close to anyone in a dating relationship again. There are no guarantees about how things will turn out, so facing the risks can be a Herculean effort. Fortunately, for those who muster the guts, there are guarantees of grace loaves at their feet.

One of the greatest sources of manna in my life comes from people around me. While everyone needs encouragement, singles especially need people who will walk with them. Regardless of the road—relationships, careers, habits, involvements—as a single adult, I don't have the built-in support system provided by a spouse. I don't have a constant someone to recognize the difficulties I face and help me find my way through them. It's a matter of survival for me to have friends who can lend faithful support and encouragement. Like fearful Moses needed Aaron, I need constant encouragements beside me, friends who see the things that make me afraid and help me move right through them. They are friends who become what Isaiah might call "pools of water" in the desert (Isa. 41:18).

There was a time in my life when I wasn't willing to let people walk so closely with me. In fact, when I was in college, I nearly lost a dear friend who was frustrated with my lack of vulnerability. I wouldn't even let the people closest to me see where I struggled, much less ask for any help.

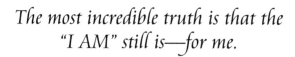

*The most incredible truth is that the
"I AM" still is—for me.*

Somewhere along the way, I learned better. I look around at several key friends now and can only imagine how horrible it would be to walk tough roads without them. They have been "gifts of Aaron" to me when I perhaps would have shrunken back from divine direction. Friends like this don't lurk behind every corner, but they are worth looking for. They are worth every ounce of vulnerability I can squeeze out, because they are the ones who push me forward when I cower in fear from the risks of relationships, new ventures, and changes.

The story of Moses is amazing. Instead of a coward running from his slithering staff in the Midian desert, he became the man who, "by faith . . . left Egypt, not fearing the king's anger" (Heb. 11:27). Instead of a shepherd begging to be left alone, Moses grew into the prophet who powerfully led a nation to freedom. Instead of a forgotten fugitive tending sheep, he became one of the most influential people in Jewish history. When Moses met the "I AM" at the burning bush, he learned who *he* was and who he could become . . . if he'd allow God to release him from the grip of rejection.

The most amazing part of the Moses story, though, isn't what happened at the burning bush. The most incredible truth is that the "I AM" still is—for me. He is an ever-present, never-changing God, who wants to pull me out of a couple of barrels, too. With His unconditional love and acceptance, He longs to release me from the vice-like grip of loneliness, inadequacy, and fear. The choice is mine. The way out is His.

6

Jacob and Joseph: Living After Rebellion

I have done nothing but underhanded, despicable, not even terribly imaginative things since I got here, but . . . I was just trying to win you, to win you back. But that doesn't excuse any of it. I'm pond scum. Well, lower, actually. I'm like the fungus that feeds on pond scum.

—Julianne, *My Best Friend's Wedding*

$\mathcal{W}$hen I was in college, a trip to Cedarville, Ohio, from Milwaukee, Wisconsin, took seven hours (five miles per hour over, one fill-up, and two bathroom stops), a little more than a tank of gas, and $2.40 in change if I took the tollway around Chicago. Two film canisters nicely held the necessary change, and if the coins were stacked in a rotation of quarter, nickel, and dime, it expedited the process of finding forty cents for each Illinois toll.

For four years I traveled to Cedarville College in the small, sleepy, southwestern Ohio town. I know the route like the insides of my eyelids on a rainy Saturday morning. While I was in school, I always drove the same way because that's the way my dad went. I faithfully rummaged through pockets and purses for loose quarters, nickels, and dimes. I religiously stacked them in empty film canisters just like my dad would do. On occasion, I even went to the bank to get twelve quarters, twelve nickels, and twelve dimes for the round-trip tolls, just in case the state of Illinois ran out of change, I suppose.

Several years after graduation, it dawned on me that I didn't have to take Interstate 294 through the sprawling Chicago suburbs. There are a number of other ways to get to the other side of the city. (The most interesting one is a missed exit and a tour of downtown.) I also discovered that I like to read the map *while* I drive and take detours if they seem like adventures. This is definitely not my dad's style. He charts his course and follows the map. Additionally, I rarely have the right amount of coinage in my car, unless it's under the seat, and that's not a maneuver I like to attempt while driving. I also learned that they do have enough change for my dollars at the tollbooths, and it only takes a couple extra seconds to get it.

While I've recklessly abandoned the example of consistency and preparedness my father set for road trips, I have not compromised on one very significant lesson he modeled for me. The shovel. I never travel in the winter (and most other times of the year, too) without my shovel. It's a really nice, lightweight, red shovel without a scratch or dent on it.

I've endured a generous bit of mockery from my friend Jason about my shovel. He wonders when the last time was that I encountered an avalanche in the Midwest. For some reason, he thinks it's one of life's more embarrassing predicaments to have to ride in a car with a shovel stashed in the trunk. He fails to understand the "don't leave home without it" allegiance I have to my shovel.

He's right. I have never used the shovel. In fact, I have never even come close to using it. It just takes up space in my trunk, mile after uneventful mile. I've given him all kinds of reasons why I need it, none of which are good enough. However, the best rationalization for its reserved place in my trunk is quite simple—my dad carries a shovel in his trunk.

I'm amazingly like my dad. Some of the similarities are hereditary, like my nose; and some are acquired, like carrying my shovel. While I have abandoned some of his routines, overall I find myself doing much of life in the same way he does. I think in his quiet, analytical way. I listen to everyone around me but am slow to let others listen to me. I process life better when I can write about it. I move with great caution, carefully weighing each decision with the seriousness of a kid with a quarter in a candy store.

An Inheritance of Deceit

Genesis tracks several generations of God's chosen people, and it's not hard to see character traits passed on through the genes. Take Jacob, for instance. He was like his mom, Rebekah. Rebekah first appears in Scripture as the sought-out wife of Isaac, promised heir of Abraham. She then makes her mark on the pages of biblical history as the first mother of twins.

After twenty years of barrenness, Rebekah finally waddled through the exhilarating and exhausting experience of a long-awaited pregnancy. She was probably surrounded by many-time moms who showered her with stories of morning sickness and midnight cravings. Sometime, though, in the course of her nine months, things started happening in Rebekah's bulging body that didn't mirror any of her friends' stories. Perplexed and frightened, she cried out to God, "Why is this happening to me?" (Gen. 25:22).

God's answer likely took Rebekah by surprise: "Two nations are in your womb, and two peoples from within you will be separated; one people will be stronger than the other, and the older will serve the younger" (Gen. 25:23). She was carrying two sons, they would not get along, and the younger one would carry the privileges usually reserved for the firstborn.

The Bible doesn't tell us if Rebekah discussed this divine revelation with Isaac or if she kept God's prophetic words to herself. We don't know for sure what she said, but we do know what she did. She favored Jacob, the younger son, while Isaac preferred Esau. Jacob was a mama's boy. He hung around the tents, learning to cook and care for the needs of a household, while his brother Esau took hunting trips with his father. Jacob was Betty Crocker, and Esau was Rambo.

Rebekah dreamed big dreams for her favored son, and one day when opportunity knocked, she answered. On this particular day, an elderly, almost blind Isaac was pondering his mortality when he called for Esau. "My son," he began. This was a moment he had lived for, the opportunity to give a paternal blessing to his favored son, his firstborn. "Go out to the open country to hunt some wild game for me. Prepare me the kind of tasty food I like and bring it to me to eat, so that I may give you my blessing before I die" (Gen. 27:3–4). This was to be a nostalgic father-son moment, the culmination of a lifetime for a proud father and the commencement of a future for a firstborn. Esau grabbed his quiver and bow and hurried for the field, eager to please his dad.

He milked life, and when schemes ran dry he found another cow.

Ear to the tent flap as Isaac talked to *his* son, Rebekah bolted into action with *her* son. According to the prenatal prophecy, Jacob was to be honored as the firstborn, and his concerned mother intended to see that he received his due. Esau had barely reached the trees when she grabbed Jacob and whispered the plan that would guarantee fulfillment of God's promise. Sneaking in ahead of Esau with two stewed goats from the family flock, borrowed clothes from his brother's closet, and still-warm goat skins on his hairless arms, Jacob would fool Isaac into blessing him instead of Esau (scary, isn't it?).

"My son," she assured an uncertain Jacob, "just do what I say" (Gen. 27:13). Rebekah was not the kind of woman who sat around waiting for life to happen to her, or to her son for that matter. She peered in the window of opportunity and created a door.

Like Mother, Like Son

Rebekah's son learned many lessons from her. Cooking and conniving went hand in hand for Jacob, it seems. In an earlier life chapter, he sold a bowl of his best stew for the price of Esau's birthright. Then later he pitted his wits against Uncle Laban and emerged a wealthier man with healthier flocks. Yes sir, Jacob was a man of action. He made life happen, and he made it happen the way he wanted. Jacob ran the race—always on the move, always alert to opportunities. He milked life, and when schemes ran dry he found another cow. He planned, executed, and reaped the benefits.

He also paid the price. Jacob's "initiative" came at a very high cost. Having driven a deeper wedge of enmity between himself and his twin, Jacob fled from home. He never saw his mother again, and he was alienated from his brother for two decades. Furthermore, his twenty-year relationship with his uncle was strained, each keeping a suspicious eye on the other. Then as his own family grew, Jacob carried on the tradition of playing favorites and acted aggressively on behalf of *his* favored son, Joseph. He stirred up a brew of hatred within his own house that would boil over to burn him.

Joseph gained Potiphar's favor through excellent work and an exceptional attitude.

Joseph, the favored son of Jacob, burst on the scene at a cocky seventeen. He was tattling on his brothers who already despised him for being the diamond in their dad's dozen. Decked out in Dad's special coat, Joseph flaunted his favored status. With an air of importance, he informed his brothers that in his field of dreams, their bundles of grain bowed to his. Even their verbal daggers of hate didn't stop Joseph from later sharing the celestial episode of the same dream; his brothers as the stars, along with the sun and moon, bowed to him. When the chance came for the brothers to erase Joseph from the family picture, they took it. Killing him was their first choice, but they settled for selling him to a caravan of foreigners traveling to far-away Egypt.

A Fresh Start for a New Generation

Sold for twenty shekels and bound by iron shackles, Joseph left his lofty dreams in a desert pit. Relocating to Egypt for the better part of his young life had not really been part of his plans. Although, I'm not really sure Joseph had *plans*. He had *dreams*. He also had an unshakable grip on the sovereign hand of God. Later in the Genesis story, he revealed what his thoughts were during the tumultuous episodes of his life, but before ever saying a word, Egyptian-bound Joseph lived what he believed. Joseph didn't sit around waiting for God to rescue him and fulfill his dreams of bowing sheaves and dipping stars. He also didn't take it upon himself to make those things happen. Instead he settled into his unlikely career as a slave in the house of Potiphar. He picked up the duster and made the house shine.

The Bible reports to us about Joseph's life in distant Egypt:

> *The Lord was with Joseph and he prospered, and he lived in the house of his Egyptian master. When his master saw that the Lord was with him and that the Lord gave him success in everything he did, Joseph found favor in his eyes. . . . So he left in Joseph's care everything he had; with Joseph in charge, he did not concern himself with anything except the food he ate.*

—Genesis 39:2–4, 6

It's clear that God was with Joseph and had His hand in the unfolding events, but I don't think that these verses are primarily about God or about Potiphar, Joseph's master. I think the statement is about Joseph. Read between the lines, and you'll find a job review for the Hebrew slave. Potiphar didn't hand his household over to a sullen, disgruntled employee. He released the reigns to his most trusted and valued servant. Joseph gained Potiphar's favor through excellent work and an exceptional attitude. For Joseph, it didn't matter that the job description didn't fit his dreams. It was the job God had placed in front of him, so he majored in it and forgot the electives.

Joseph's hard work didn't seem to count for much, though, when Potiphar's wife entered the story. She, like every other Egyptian woman with eyes, noticed her husband's "well-built and handsome" servant, and she batted her long lashes when he was around. Actually, according to the story, she didn't bother much with batting lashes; she got right to the point. In her first scriptural appearance, she makes the less-than-subtle statement, "Come to bed with me!" (Gen. 39:7).

Wisely Joseph turned her down—repeatedly. "How then could I do such a wicked thing and sin against God?" (Gen. 39:9). Ms. Potiphar was not accustomed to being refused by anyone, much less a foreign slave, so she made sure Joseph paid for his insolence. She shredded his resume, and Joseph was sent directly to jail without any chance to collect his reputation.

Once again in captivity, Joseph eyed an unwelcome vegetable on his plate, and once again instead of banging his silverware on the table in protest, he dived in and devoured it ravenously. The Bible tells it like this:

But while Joseph was there in the prison, the Lord was with him; he showed him kindness and granted him favor in the eyes of the prison warden. So the warden put Joseph in charge of all those held in the prison, and he was made responsible for all that was done there. The warden paid no attention to anything under Joseph's care. . . .

—Genesis 39:20–23

Faced with another job that wasn't on anyone's ladder to success, Joseph wholeheartedly climbed the repulsive rungs.

Driving Through the Fog

One summer shortly after my conversion to the Church of the Football Channel, I took a road trip by myself to Green Bay to see the sites of Packerland, USA. With my map in my lap, I left home and headed north on a highway that was nearly hidden in a deep fog. Road signs were covered with low clouds and were impossible to read. At that time, I hadn't ever been to Green Bay, but I had a general idea where I was going. North. How hard could that be? So, in spite of the dense fog, I kept my eyes on what I could see of the road, maintained an even speed, and drove in the direction of my destination.

After several miles of driving in the misty blur, the fog lifted and the sun came out. Finally I could read the road signs and confirm that, indeed, I was going the right way. Not too far down the road the fog fell again, blanketing me in blindness. Confident that my map was good and my direction was correct, I again kept my eyes on the road and maintained an even speed. The rise and fall of fog continued for most of the two-hour journey.

When I made that trip, I was three days away from a career change. After nearly a full year of God's tedious, but timely, leading, I knew I was going in the right direction. He had marked the road so clearly for me that I had no doubt about the future. However, confidence in His direction doesn't necessarily pave a sunny street. The new position sent me into the fog on an unknown road.

God led me out of a job I did well and mostly enjoyed into a position I struggled to do and mostly didn't enjoy. There were sunny patches along the road when I thought I was finally beginning to understand His plan, but no sooner would the sun warm me up than the fog would descend again. The rise and fall of fog continued for most of the two-year journey.

In the stretches of thickest fog, a dear friend traveled with me. He listened to me struggle with the blindness and describe "black cloud days," those darkest of days when life just looms, situations are suffocating, and confusion is constant. He lovingly listened and tried to understand, but he wasn't driving. The passenger seat is only a few feet away from the driver's side, but the pressures of each place are often miles apart.

God doesn't need help accomplishing His plans. In His time and in His way, He gets the job done without the painful ripples of rebellion.

One of his favorite words is "proactive." It's the way he lives, attacking life with enthusiasm and purpose. It's frustrating to him when people seem to live in neutral, lazily letting life happen to them. I think he sometimes listened to my fog reports with a little bit of frustration, wondering if I couldn't *do* something to make the situation better. He asked if I should send out resumes or start considering other positions. All I could tell him was, "I know I'm in the right place. It doesn't make sense to me and I don't like a lot about it. But until God uncovers a road sign pointing in another direction, I don't *want* to be anywhere else." I knew that God was up to something, and I knew that in His perfect time the fog would lift.

The Way to Wait

Joseph's life reads like my trip to Green Bay and my career journeys. Sunshine, fog, sunshine, fog. His worst "black cloud day" came when he did a favor for the imprisoned cupbearer of Pharaoh, and then was forgotten by the released resident of the palace. He was left, instead, to etch another seven hundred thirty marks in the prison wall.

The Bible doesn't track Joseph's actions during those two years, but I imagine he did what he had learned to do well as he traveled from pit to palace to prison—wait on God to work through the adversity. In all of his travels, Joseph had learned lessons about life that his dad, Jacob, hadn't: God doesn't need help accomplishing His plans. In His time and in His way, He gets the job done without the painful ripples of rebellion.

There's a huge difference between *waiting* and *waiting on God.* Waiting is passing the time, wondering and worrying about what might happen. It's wishing upon a stationary star while the world keeps turning. Waiting on God is proactively living in the middle of His ordained circumstances, confident of purpose in the process. It's running the race even when every muscle aches and every limb throbs.

The unpopular truth is that God often does His greatest work while we wait. It's when He puts us in prison, when He traps us inside the cold, clammy walls of a stone cell, that He gives us the greatest opportunity to experience His deliverance. Just ask the descendants of Joseph, centuries later.

Hang On and Keep Moving

Exodus 13 records the Hebrew slaves' journey from the unbearable bondage of Egypt to the shores of the Red Sea. With Egyptian dust still on their shoes, the Israelites were headed to the Promised Land on the heels of the worst night in Egyptian history. Death had crept through the country, and an angry, grief-stricken Pharaoh had ordered the Israelites out. They grabbed their belongings, rushed out of Goshen, and began their desert journey. Undoubtedly for the first few miles, they cast anxious eyes over their shoulders, wondering if this was too good to be true. Soon, though, the stretches of sand swept away their four-century-old nightmare. By Exodus 14:8, the people were "marching out boldly," the Promised Land within their scope of imagination. They were free.

The Bible clearly says that God took them the way He did, even though it wasn't the shortest route. He led them straight to the shore of the Red Sea. Confidence was high as the former slaves swapped sphinx stories around campfires and laughed at the mere memory of bondage.

Then they heard it. The distant sound of thundering chariots. The ominous pounding of Pharaoh's furious army. Sizing up their situation in an instant, the Israelites knew they were trapped. The water in front, the strength of the world behind. What had happened to their dream? What had happened to God's plan? Hadn't they followed His cloud-fire pillar? Hadn't they marked their route by His road map? "What have you done to us by bringing us out of Egypt?" they screamed in terror at Moses (Exod. 14:11). Hope that was only hours old disappeared in a deluge of familiar despair.

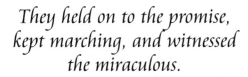

> *They held on to the promise,*
> *kept marching, and witnessed*
> *the miraculous.*

The only answer Moses could give was, "Do not be afraid. Stand firm and you will see the deliverance the LORD will bring you today. . . . The LORD will fight for you" (Exod. 14:13–14). Did Moses have a plan? No. All he had was a promise and a dream of freedom. And that was enough. "Hang in there," was all Moses could tell the paralyzed people. "God is on your side."

Holding on to the promises got them through the night, but it wouldn't have gotten them to the Promised Land. "Tell the Israelites to move on," ordered God, already preparing the way for them (Exod. 14:15). During the night the sea waters parted, and in the morning the frightened people marched. They moved, but not because they saw the ultimate victory. They kept marching because the alternative was unthinkable.

You know the rest of the story. The people of God crossed to the other side, the Egyptians raced into the Red Sea after them, and God pulled the plug. The formidable foe was washed away as the God of Israel displayed His incredible power. And the people of God wondered what they ever worried about. They held on to the promise, kept marching, and witnessed the miraculous.

They had a little bit of "Father Joseph" in them. Joseph, seasoned veteran of the trapped situation, had spent perilous hours at the bottom of a pit while his brothers bartered away his comfortable life. He'd curled up in the corner of an Egyptian jail while his name was stained with juice from the palace grapevine. When his dreams seemed more like a joke, a mockery to a man mistreated, mistrusted, and misused, Joseph waited on God and kept moving.

And how the waters parted! Joseph wept as he watched his boyhood vision of submissive stars explode into a galaxy of God's greatness. God raised Joseph to second-in-command in Egypt. He gave him a wife. He blessed him with two sons. He provided the ultimate job. He brought his brothers back. And the brightest star in the cluster? God reunited Joseph and Jacob; He put father and son back together again. "As soon as Joseph appeared before [Jacob], he threw his arms around his father and wept for a long time" (Gen. 46:29).

The End of the Road

It's out of those final years together in Egypt that both Jacob and Joseph are commended for their faith.

> *By faith Joseph, when his end was near, spoke about the exodus of the Israelites from Egypt and gave instructions about his bones.*
>
> —Hebrews 11:22

Joseph had learned to take life as God served it, recognizing that a masterpiece includes dark strokes.

Of all the things in Joseph's remarkable life, it seems un-usual that God isolated his last words as the mark of his faith. The more I've studied his story, though, the more these words seem to summarize his entire life. Joseph was a man who had known the best of times and the worst of times. He had eaten with prison rats and palace royalty. Joseph had learned to take life as God served it, recogniz-ing that a masterpiece includes dark strokes. The black clouds of adversity had formed the backdrop of his life, defining his godly character and highlighting his personal holiness.

His words to his brothers when they discovered him alive in Egypt shout his confidence in God, "It was to save lives that *God sent me* ahead of you. . . . But *God sent me* ahead of you . . . So then, *it was not you who sent me here, but God*" (Gen. 45:5–8, emphasis mine). Sometime later he reassured them again with his perspective on God's plan, "You in-tended to harm me, but God intended it for good to ac-complish what is now being done" (Gen. 50:20). Even when his circumstances stunk, Joseph knew that God was still involved.

As he approached death, Joseph spoke words reflecting the faith that had made up his life. He foresaw tough days for the people of God in the land of Egypt, but he also saw the bigger plan of God. "But God will surely come to your aid and take you up out of this land to the land He promised on oath to Abraham, Isaac, and Jacob. . . . God will surely come to your aid, and then you must carry my bones up from this place" (Gen. 50:24–25). Joseph knew that Egyptian slavery was part of God's plan for His people, but he also knew there was a Promised Land in their future, too. The God who sent them to Egypt would also lead them out of Egypt. He would be faithful, accompanying them every step of the painful way. Joseph had walked his own painful way in partnership with the same God.

Jacob is commended for his faith in blessing his two grandchildren, Manasseh and Ephraim. "By faith Jacob, when he was dying, blessed each of Joseph's sons, and worshiped as he leaned on the top of his staff" (Heb. 11:21).

The blessing of Manasseh and Ephraim bears surreal similarities to another time and place. Mostly blind and approaching death, Jacob called for his favored son and two grandchildren. "Bring them to me so that I may bless them," he said to Joseph (Gen. 48:9). With a child perched on each aging knee, Jacob tightly held the boys he never dreamed would even exist. "I never expected to see *your* face again," he said to Joseph, "and now God has allowed me to see your children too" (48:11, emphasis mine). What a moment!

Joseph took his sons from his father's lap and stood them in front of him to receive his blessing. He carefully positioned Manasseh, the older brother, on Jacob's right side to receive the firstborn's blessing, while little Ephraim was placed at his grandfather's left side. The elderly patriarch carefully reached out his *right hand* and placed it on *Ephraim's* head. Crossing his arms, he then put his *left hand* on firstborn *Manasseh's* head. As he uttered his blessing on the boys and their father, Jacob was interrupted by his displeased son.

Thinking his absentminded father had forgotten which grandson was which, Joseph grabbed Jacob's right hand and tried to move it to Manasseh's head instead. "No, my father," he insisted, "*this* one is the firstborn; put your right hand on *his* head" (Gen. 48:18, emphasis mine).

While he couldn't see much in front of him, at that moment Jacob saw everything behind him. He smelled Isaac's favorite goat-dish; he felt the prickle of animal hair on his smooth arms; he even bent a little under the weight of his husky brother's clothes. Jacob grasped the significance of that long-ago deception like he never had before. Standing at his feet was a piece of his future, a sampling of those who would carry on the family name. With regret he probably wished he had a better legacy to leave them.

He'd forfeited the inexplicable joy of seeing God make the impossible happen every step of the way.

Turning to an indignant Joseph, Jacob refused to move his hand. He looked at his lost-and-found son, sighed deeply, and spoke gentle words soaked with experience, "I know, my son, I know" (Gen. 48:19). Indeed he knew. For the first recorded time in his life, Jacob did things *God's* way instead of manipulating them *his* way. As the scenes of his life flashed across his mind, he remembered the pain he'd caused by taking matters in his own hands. He remembered the sorrow he'd endured because he couldn't wait for God to carry out His promises. Perhaps he wistfully wondered how God would have solved things if he had only stayed out of it. A stubborn schemer, Jacob perhaps didn't recognize his own helplessness until he lost Joseph. When his favored son was reported dead, Jacob entered new territory; for once the circumstances were beyond his manipulation. In the ensuing years of absence, Jacob discovered God in a new way. In the prison of his pain, he pondered his life and the choices he had made. When God did the miraculous by bringing Joseph "back from the dead" and reunited father and son, Jacob fully understood all that he had missed in life. He'd forfeited the inexplicable joy of seeing God make the impossible happen every step of the way.

I don't ever want to sit in Jacob's seat. The frustration and pain of being single is nothing compared to the frustration and pain I would cause by meddling in God's business. My life is His work. I am His workmanship. He's in the middle of an incredible masterpiece, and only eternity will reveal the full extent of His plan. In the meantime, I'm going to keep my eyes on the road, maintain an even speed, and head in the right direction.

7

Cain and Abel: Living in Worship

Well, I mean, I do like things the way I like them, but who doesn't, and anyway in my life I'm the only one who ever does anything. So what does it matter?

—Melanie, *One Fine Day*

*T*ammy and I are good tenants. We pay our rent on time, and we don't play loud music at midnight. In spite of our good behavior, Mike the Manager thinks we're a couple of dingbats. Our apartment is directly above his, which unfortunately provides ample ammunition for his theory.

One winter the overhead light in our kitchen burned out repeatedly. Since changing it required standing on a chair and unscrewing a glass dish, we didn't fight each other to replace the burned out bulb every other week. Instead we got used to the dark.

The nature of single life demands self-sufficiency.

Our friend Adam arrived early one weekend to help us get ready for a party. We pointed him in the direction of the vacuum cleaner, and when he finished cleaning the carpet, we asked him to change the kitchen light bulb. While Adam stood on the chair, we told him that the light seemed to burn out frequently. He took a closer look at the fixture and noticed it was corroded. "You guys need a new light fixture. Tell the manager about this one," he advised.

Since our kitchen was well lit again, we ignored his advice. A couple of weeks later, the garbage disposal broke, meriting a phone call downstairs. While Mike the Manager fixed the disposal, I mentioned that we needed a new kitchen light fixture. He asked some managerial questions like "Why?" and "What's wrong with it?" which of course I didn't exactly know since I hadn't even looked at it. Instead of laboriously explaining the story of Adam and our party, I simply said to him, "The guy who changes our light bulbs said we need a new fixture. It's corroded or something." All over his face I could read it: "They have a guy who changes their light bulbs? Dingbats."

Several weeks later, Tammy was hanging a curtain rod in the living room. In our apartment, a butter knife doubles as a screwdriver and a hard-heeled shoe makes a decent hammer. For the curtain rod job, though, Tammy decided she needed a screwdriver that didn't also spread butter. She went downstairs to borrow one from Mike the Manager. He looked at her with a generous amount of skepticism. Really, it's no surprise; tenants who can't change their own light bulbs shouldn't be trusted with tools. Mike probably wonders how girls who do household repairs and assemble furniture with butter knives manage to hold down real jobs. He'd find it hard to believe that we're both incredibly self-sufficient. We're independent, accomplished, and capable single adults.

A Declaration of Independence

Independence is more than the American way for singles; it's a survival skill. We do things for ourselves because there's no one else to do them for us. No one carries groceries, balances the checkbook, pumps gas, or opens doors. If we want something done, we're the ones to do it. An elderly lady once reprimanded me for moving some boxes, saying "Moving boxes is a man's job." She may be right, but I'd grow concrete cobwebs waiting for a man to move all the boxes in my life. The nature of single life demands self-sufficiency.

While it seems to be the key to single living, in reality self-sufficiency unlocks a dangerous door to self-destruction. Because I take care of myself when it comes to laundry, phone bills, and decent meals, I easily assume responsibility for all of my life. I know what my needs are, and I am capable of meeting them. I choose to do things my way, and there's seemingly no one to protest. Except God, the One who designed me to need Him; the One who knows I'm lost without Him.

Wrestling with self-sufficiency is not a modern dilemma, and it's not a struggle exclusive to singles. Humanity has engaged in the battle for control since our earliest days on this fallen planet. The fight against God's sovereign claim on His creation goes all the way back to the first family. The story of Adam, Eve, Cain, and Abel introduces the ramifications of self-sufficiency.

The First Family

Adam and Eve are the only parents in history who didn't walk uphill both ways to school barefoot through three feet of snow. The popular parental series, "When I Was a Kid," was not in their repertoire of bedtime stories. Like all parents, however, they probably told their two sons, Cain and Abel, stories about the "good old days." They are, in fact, the only parents in history whose claim on the "good old days" can't be disputed. Life in the Garden of Eden had been perfect. For two wonderful chapters in Genesis, crumbs of a delectable dessert fall on the plates of our imaginations; for a lifetime the children of Adam and Eve feasted on the crumbs that fell from the plates of their parents' memories.

It's easy to imagine Adam taking his little boys to the edge of the Garden where an angel wielding a flaming sword stood. Perhaps he told tales about life inside that secret, unreachable place. As his sons grew, it's likely that he and Cain sweat together coaxing the ground to bring forth a crop. While Adam longed aloud for the weedless soil of Eden, Cain probably grinned at his dad's lip-smacking descriptions of the succulent fruit and crisp vegetables in the Garden. Maybe as Adam and Abel tended stubborn sheep on the hillside, Abel laughed at his dad's account of why a sheep was a "sheep" and not an "ostrich" or a "kangaroo." I can picture both boys shaking their heads in disbelief at their father's claim to have once perfectly understood the workings of his wife's mind.

While Adam and Eve undoubtedly told many stories *to* their boys, the Bible itself only includes one story *about* their boys. Their brief appearance is enough, however, to make a sobering statement about humanity. From the contents of that one story, Cain is condemned for his malevolence, and Abel is commended for his faith.

> *By faith Abel offered God a better sacrifice than Cain did. By faith he was commended as a righteous man, when God spoke well of his offerings. And by faith he still speaks, even though he is dead.*
>
> —Hebrews 11:4

The Birth of Death

Abel flits across the page in Genesis like an autumn leaf. Caught in a whirlwind, he barely touches the page of chapter four long enough to be recognized before he's borne away on a chilly breeze. The second child of Adam and Eve, Abel came crying into a world that, like his own parents, still remembered what it was like to be perfect. Wilted flowers, dried grass, and dominating weeds seemed like foreigners crowding out the natives. Death, the product of Eden's sin, pinched like a new shoe.

When Genesis chapter 4 opens, that shoe was still unworn by people. "For dust you are and to dust you will return," was a certainty connected to the curse in chapter 3, but it hadn't happened yet. The death of a human being was a great unknown. Adam and Eve knew "it" would happen, but they had no idea exactly what "it" meant. God Himself had never dealt with the death of a human being either. The destruction of His masterfully designed creation, the extinguishing of His very breath, the crumbling of His image-bearers—certainly God dreaded the awful day more than His creation ever could.

When the chapter closes, the cycle of life and death had completed its first round. Abel was dead, killed by the soil-stained hands of his own brother. Cain was sentenced to a life of restless wandering apart from what was left of his family. Adam and Eve lost two sons in one day. Their minds must have throbbed with memories of their sweet baby Cain, the first baby ever to have his fingers and toes counted by awestruck parents. When Abel was born, they marveled all over again at the wonder of God's tiny "almost-perfect" creation. Never in those moments could they have grasped how far from perfect they really were. Eden was just over the hill, and its memories were even closer. They must have reeled in horror as they saw the bloody result of their choice in the Garden so many years before. The devastation of death, the loss of a loved one, division in the family—they had planted the seeds for the horrible events of that day.

The pitiful truth of humanity is that we quickly stumble into sin without any assistance.

The impact of death in the post-Eden years is incomprehensible to us, who watch violence for entertainment, expect the night's top story to border on brutality, and sporadically attend the funerals of friends and relatives. In the world we know, death is as much a part of life as birth. After several thousand years of life on a sinful planet, we aren't shocked anymore at the ugliness of sin. We don't like it, but it's the way of life in a fallen world.

One of the more staggering truths locked in the account

of Cain and Abel is that it took place in Genesis instead of Isaiah, Jeremiah, or some other late book. Less than five pages into my Bible, this dreadful event occurred. It didn't take very long for mankind to plunge to the depths of depravity. You'd like to think we would have slowly worked our way into worse and worse sins, finally, after years of practice, achieving a state of total moral decadence. Instead, the pitiful truth of humanity is that we quickly stumble into sin without any assistance. The murder of Abel wasn't prompted by violence on television, and it wasn't instigated by a street gang. There was no scarred childhood to blame, no ills of society to account for the horror of Genesis 4.

A Matter of the Heart

How did things go so wrong, so fast?

The murder of Abel began with an act of worship. The story opens with both sons coming to the Lord with sacrifices. "Cain brought some of the fruits of the soil. . . . But Abel brought fat portions from some of the firstborn of his flock" (Gen. 4:3–4). Nothing else is said about the actual sacrifices. All we know is that the Lord looked on Abel's offering with favor, while He saw Cain's sacrifice as unacceptable.

God doesn't tell us specifically what was wrong with Cain's offering. Some have suggested that Cain needed to bring an animal for a blood sacrifice, but later biblical instruction makes it clear that grain offerings were acceptable at times. Another thought is that Cain didn't bring God his best. The passage states what he brought, and then draws a contrast by saying "but Abel brought . . ." Cain brought some of his crop, but Abel picked his best sheep.

*Somewhere between acne remedies
and cheerleading tryouts, I began to
understand that most worship
doesn't happen anywhere
near church on Sunday.*

There's more to this story than what went up in flames.
If the objects on the altars were the focus of the passage,
God would have added a few more details for our understanding. The story isn't about prize-winning sheep and
slightly bruised produce. It's about worship.

I'm the product of a Baptist Sunday school, and as a child,
I learned about worship. Simply stated, worship is having
reverence and honor for God. While that sounds pretty
simple, worship, reverence, and honor are tough abstract
words for young concrete minds to absorb. My Sunday school
teachers explained it in terms of action—singing songs, giving pennies, attending church, saying prayers, reading verses.
Worship fit very nicely into the Sunday morning interlude
called "church." In fact, in my mental childhood dictionary,
"worship" and "church" were synonymous.

During my short stay in the Primary Department, I faithfully worshiped, memorizing verses, doing weekly lessons,
and contributing great poundage to penny contests. When
I moved to the Junior Department, I continued in the prescribed pattern of behavior, reigning as queen of Bible baseball, "sword drills," and perfect attendance. I moved from
grade level to grade level, department to department, worshiping God as I'd been taught. Somewhere between acne

remedies and cheerleading tryouts, I began to understand that most worship doesn't happen anywhere near church on Sunday. It flows out of the heart on Monday through Saturday. I figured out that worship is always about the heart; it's never about spiritual practices or accomplishments.

Two Pairs of Glasses

Romans 12:1–2 explains it by saying to "offer your bodies as living sacrifices, holy and pleasing to God—*this is your spiritual worship*. Do not conform any longer to the pattern of this world, but be transformed by the renewing of your mind" (emphasis mine). It sounds pretty simple. Live every day to please God. Don't do the things the world does. Focus on Him.

It's the hardest thing I *try* every day. What makes it so difficult is that I've got terrible eyesight. Like every other descendant of Adam and Eve, my view of the world is blurred. I look in the mirror and don't see myself clearly. I come away thinking that I look much better than I really do. I look at God, and He appears to be fairly small and unessential to my daily life. I suffer, along with the rest of the human race, from an out-of-focus perspective on reality.

Even as a blood-bought child of God,
I wake up every day, look in the mirror,
and tend to think I'm pretty okay.

Reality is that I am a rotten-to-the-core sinner. Depravity goes deep. Sin flows from the core of each human being, making individual capacity for evil frightening. It doesn't matter who I am, who my parents are, where I grew up, or how much education I have; I am capable of engaging in the vilest of sins.

Reality is that God defies description. His amazing grace is the theme of history. He is so big that I can't begin to comprehend Him, and yet the marvel is that He lets me know Him. He stooped from His universal throne to reveal Himself. Knowing the despicable condition of my heart, He still invited me to join His family.

Unfortunately, accepting His gift of salvation didn't fix my eyesight. Even as a blood-bought child of God, I wake up every day, look in the mirror, and tend to think I'm pretty okay. I survey my day's responsibilities, glance in God's direction, and quickly dismiss my need for assistance. Reverencing and honoring God are important to me, but very quickly I slot them into the week and dedicate the rest of the time to myself. Just like Cain.

I don't want to be like Cain. I want to be what Paul urged in Romans 12:1–2. So every morning when I get up, I try to remember to put on two pairs of glasses. First, I wear the pair prescribed by my eye doctor to fix my astigmatic and nearsighted vision. There's never a day that I decide I don't need to wear my glasses just because I wore them the day before. They are not medicinal, curing my defective eyes. They are corrective and only help me see better when I actually wear them. In this lifetime, I will not outgrow my need for corrective lenses. One of the small joys of eternity is the knowledge that I won't have glasses slipping down my nose or pinching behind my ears.

The second pair of glasses that I need to put on are my God-glasses, my lenses of worship. Worship takes me to the feet of God, where looking up, I glimpse an all-powerful

God whose glory fills the earth. When I turn to view myself in the mirror, the blur clears. I am small and weak; I am sinful and stubborn. I am not the independent, self-sufficient, accomplished single adult I'd like to think. Seeing God enlarges my vulnerability. It sharpens my focus on reality. God is great, I am small, and here's the shocker: He loves me anyway. If Romans 12:1 is to be reality, every day I must see Him clearly and see myself accurately. Just because I worshiped yesterday doesn't mean I can skip it today.

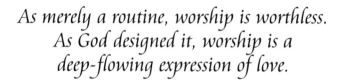

As merely a routine, worship is worthless.
As God designed it, worship is a
deep-flowing expression of love.

Worship may not be a cure-all for my sinful tendencies, but, unlike my prescription lenses, it does progressively change my vision. As I faithfully wear my God-glasses, He changes my perspective. When I draw close to Him in regular worship, He perfects me into the image of Jesus; I see Him more clearly, and I see myself in relation to Him.

Throughout history, God has provided glasses for His children to wear to see Him and themselves more clearly. For Old Testament followers, He established the sacrificial system of worship. The perfect animals and the shed blood reminded them of their sin and His forgiveness. He designed feasts and celebrations for them to enjoy. Each event commemorated His miraculous work on their rebellious behalf. He instituted the practice of tithing, reminding each giver of the source of wealth. In the New

Testament, Jesus modeled and mandated baptism, an identification with God's plan. He left His followers with the Lord's Table, a solemn remembrance of His death and resurrection.

The Heart of the Matter

God never intended for acts of worship to become spiritual duties. As much as I like to think that my input matters, the Almighty doesn't need my resources nor is He impressed by what I choose to give Him. Instead, God is delighted when my worship flows from a heart beating steadily for Him. As merely a routine, worship is worthless. As God designed it, worship is a deep-flowing expression of love.

Cain's sacrifice was unacceptable because his heart was unacceptable. Somewhere in the depths of his depraved heart, Cain decided that he didn't need God. He went through the motions of worship, assuming it would be enough for the small God he saw through blurred eyes. He performed his religious duty, and when he looked in the mirror, he looked even better than he'd first thought. Cain flat-lined the heart check. He was a worshiping corpse.

The sadder part of the story is that God offered him a chance to come back to life, but he chose to stay in the coffin. When God rejected his sacrifice, Cain faced a choice. He could have put his God-glasses on, recognized his sin, and repented. He could have let the spiritual defibrillator jump-start his heart. Instead he angrily brushed aside God's diagnosis. Scripture says Cain was very angry. He was angry with a God who had the audacity to reject his sacrifice. He was angry with a brother who made him look bad. He was angry with the Sovereign who saw through his charade.

A long-suffering God looked at the hostile worshiper and instead of striking him dead for rebellion, He went straight to the heart of the issue.

> *Why are you angry? Why is your face downcast? If you do what is right, will you not be accepted? But if you do not do what is right, sin is crouching at your door; it desires to have you, but you must master it.*
>
> —Genesis 4:6–7

God called Cain's worship bluff, essentially saying, "You've done the wrong thing. Admit it, and let's move on." He extended an invitation to repent, and then He went a step further, offering Cain some godly advice about the dangerous monster of sin.

The Bogeyman and the Basement

The basement of the house in which I grew up had monsters. They lurked in dark corners waiting for foolhardy children to venture into their domain. Like basement monsters everywhere, they were inactive during the day and only posed a threat after dark. Unless absolutely necessary, I avoided the basement at night.

All houses are designed by adults, those fortunate people who are never the prey of basement monsters. With no thought for the safety of their children, my parents placed the family game closet at the foot of the basement steps. On rare evenings when I persuaded someone to play a board game with me, I had to grit my teeth and enter the land of the monsters to get it. I'd creep stealthily down the steps, carefully avoiding the creaky places so as not to alert the basement inhabitants of my approach. Reaching the bottom step, I'd take a deep breath, open the door, and step into the darkness. At this point in the game search, everything happened quickly. I'd hastily close the basement door in order to reach the game closet behind it. Pulling open the cabinet doors, I'd grab the closest game, slam the doors, and race up the steps to safety.

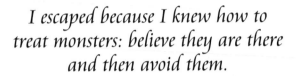

I escaped because I knew how to treat monsters: believe they are there and then avoid them.

I'm happy to say the monsters never got me. I know they crouched in every corner, just waiting for me to stumble close enough to be snatched. I escaped because I knew how to treat monsters: believe they are there and then avoid them. I never met a monster face-to-face, but I knew their danger, and I respected their existence. Furthermore, I never teased them or wandered close to their corners. I stayed as far away as I could.

Cain didn't have monsters in his basement; he had far worse. The monsters of evil lurked just outside the door of his decisions. "Sin is crouching at your door; it desires to have you, but you must master it" (Gen. 4:7). Tossing aside God's clear warning, Cain walked boldly in the direction of sin. He threw himself into the waiting arms of the murderous monster, never even attempting to avoid it, much less master it. With his own hands, he pummeled the life out of his brother. Righteous Abel died because of self-righteous Cain.

It's not hard to be overtaken by monsters. All it takes is an arrogant saunter into their territory. Monsters don't chase proud people; they just wait for them to show up. Cain, blind to his own weakness, assumed he was strong enough to take care of himself in the face of demonic danger. He thought he was exempt from the warnings of God.

When God again opened his hand for Cain to confess by asking, "Where is your brother Abel?" Cain scorned Him. He should have fallen apart in horror at what his hands had done, but instead, we hear his angry answer spat in the face of God. "I don't know. Am I my brother's keeper?" (Gen. 4:9).

I wonder how the story would have been different if Cain had broken down in repentance. Sadly, he never did. He protested God's severe punishment but never acknowledged the horrific deed he had committed. He refused to see his sin and was unwilling to admit that sin had mastered him. Cain made the rules for his life—about everything from his sacrifice to his sibling. He lived in a state of self-sufficiency. He was all he needed.

Life apart from God is restless wandering.

So God gave him what he wanted—himself. God uprooted Cain from his home and banished him from his family. He cursed the very ground from which Cain had brought his measly sacrifice; it would no longer produce crops for him. God took away his family, his home, and his livelihood. Cain was left with himself and a lifetime to pursue fulfillment and satisfaction where it could never be found. "So Cain went out from the LORD's presence and lived in the land of Nod, east of Eden" (4:16). When he chose life apart from God, he also forfeited all peace and purpose for the rest of his days. Life apart from God is restless wandering.

Home Is Where the Heart Is

God never intended for the prize of His creation to wander through life apart from Him. He made us instead to find our home *in* Him. Several centuries later, Moses, nomad extraordinaire, called God our dwelling place, the place and person in whom we find meaning (Psalm 90).

God wants us to be like the turtle I saw crossing the highway one afternoon. When I passed him at fifty-five miles per hour (okay, maybe fifty-nine miles per hour), he had just crossed the on-ramp and was about to enter three lanes of breakneck traffic. He had wandered from the safety of the swamp to enter life in the fast lane, but he never really left home. He took it with him, like a turtle does everywhere he goes. A turtle's shell is more than just his permanent residence; it's part of his very existence. Apart from it, a turtle is just a heap of fragmented limbs, organs, and bones—useless, helpless, wasted.

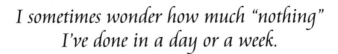

I sometimes wonder how much "nothing"
I've done in a day or a week.

In John 15:4–5, Jesus told His followers to be like that turtle: "Abide in me, and I in you. . . . For without me ye can do nothing" (KJV). At salvation, Christ establishes our eternal address in heaven, but He also summons us to Himself, our daily dwelling place on earth. He is our source of safety and protection, and more importantly, our source of life itself. Apart from Him, our efforts are wasted. They are nothing. Moses recognized the emptiness of his efforts when he concluded Psalm 90: "Establish the work of our hands for us—yes, establish the work of our hands." Only God makes it count.

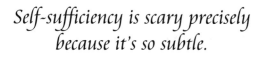

> *Self-sufficiency is scary precisely because it's so subtle.*

I sometimes wonder how much "nothing" I've done in a day or a week. How many times do I make my way through the days as just a fragmented heap of human effort? How many times do I bypass daily, momentary decisions to abide in Him—to think as He thinks, to want what He wants, to do what He'd do? How often do I tear myself away from the very thing that holds me together? How often do I try to move without my dwelling place going with me?

I've learned over the years that I can skip devotions, hurry through prayer, and mouth the words to choruses without my life falling apart. When I pillow my pious head after a day of mindless "worship," I don't entertain thoughts of murdering my sister (she's very glad about this). Instead I usually applaud myself for giving God more than His fair share of weekend time. I can get away with a certain amount of lethargic spiritual living without anyone else seeing the effects. In fact, sometimes I think I can get away with a certain amount of lethargic spiritual living without there being any effects at all. That's a masterful lie of Satan, convincing me that I'm okay just the way I am. I can be self-sufficient.

Self-sufficiency is scary precisely because it's so subtle. I don't wake up and consciously decide that I'm enough. I don't dress for church with the intention of mocking God. Instead I make little decisions that quietly say "I don't need God for this. I'll be okay." My heart whispers the words, but my mouth never gives voice to them. I'll *always* tell you that I need God. I'll always tell you that I can't do anything on my own. But that's not what I always do. There are too many hours when I choose to live apart from Him. There are too many days when I leave my God-glasses safely on the shelf, while I do a whole lot of nothing all day.

Bad News and Good News

I'll give you the bad news first. Single adults get to "go it alone." I'm told that life can be more difficult after the exchange of rings and vows, and while I'm sure this is true, I still envy something my married friends have. Marriage provides a built-in accountability partner, someone who made a vow before God to care for the emotional, spiritual, and physical needs of a mate. I know this doesn't always happen, but I envy the *opportunity* for it to happen. In God's Edenic design, man and woman are partnered together to accompany each other through life's ups and downs. They are to become one in heart, body, and mind. Living that way gives a spouse ready access to the little things. It's significantly easier, I think, to get away with little things as a single. There's no one to know the intimate secrets of my life unless I choose to put such a person in place.

And that's the good news. I can choose not to "go it

alone." God may have created man and woman to join together, but that's not the only institution He so carefully
designed. He invented the church, the family of believers
who are responsible for and accountable to one another.

If I am to successfully lock the door on lurking monsters,
I must be willing to hand the keys to someone else. I need
someone to look me in the face and say, "Where are your
glasses?" I need someone to grab my arm and say, "I sense a
weak spiritual pulse. Let me help you." A trusted friend
must have access to the details of my daily living, and they
must have permission to ask tough questions.

Maybe you need to meet with someone once a week. Perhaps you should be doing a Bible study with a friend. Maybe
you need a phone call every day. I don't know how it works
for you. I just know it has to work. You've got a vicious
beast just outside your door, and unless someone is helping
you master it, the monster will grab you.

And if you don't? If you choose to go it alone? It's not
likely you'll turn into the next Jeffrey Dahmer. You probably won't embezzle millions of dollars. You may not fall
into gross immorality. It's not likely, but as sure as you're
related to Cain, it's possible. Admit the horror of where you
could go, and then take a good look at the little things. Too
quickly, little lapses grow into big beasts.

Be a turtle with glasses. Live and move about in the
Dwelling Place you were designed to inhabit. Wear the
glasses that help you see a big God and a small self. Restless wandering and spiritual blindness were never God's plan
for you.

8

Enoch: Living with Purpose

Dear Friend, I like to start my notes to you as if we're already in the middle of a conversation. I pretend that we're the oldest and dearest of friends, as opposed to what we actually are—people who don't know each other's names and met in a chat room where we both claimed we'd never been before.

—Kathleen Kelly, *You've Got Mail*

*E*vergreen Cemetery botched the one thing it's in business to do—bury bodies. After visiting the grave site of her son for over a year, Geraldine Williamson learned that he was not buried in that spot. A grave digger pointed her in the direction of another site. Shaken and concerned about the error, Ms. Williamson initiated the unearthing and exhumation of two bodies, neither of which were her son. On the third attempt, she finally found his remains. Her appalling discovery only added momentum to an avalanche of complaints already leveled against the cemetery. Dozens of other suspicious families found themselves victims of the same administrative debacle as they searched for their misplaced loved ones.

Enoch is the picture of a purposeful life.

Pending the return of Jesus, someday I'll own a little piece of earth and heaven at the same time. A cold marble slab will mark the patch of grass where my bones are stored, and maybe my relatives will stop by every once in a while to reflect on my life. Since I won't get a chance then, I'd like to tell them now—if you ever discover my bones are in the wrong place, don't sweat it. I don't really care. My brittle bones and shriveled skin won't matter then. What's more important to me is what's left above the ground. I care more about the epitaph etched on my tombstone, regardless of whose bones are underneath it. I care more about the epitaph engraved on the lives of those who knew me, regardless of where my body is.

An Eternal Epitaph

Except for the fact that he didn't have one, Enoch's tombstone would have had the best epitaph ever. Enoch is one of two men who never died. Hebrews 11:5 says, "By faith Enoch was taken from this life, so that he did not experience death; he could not be found, because God had taken him away." Because of his faith, Enoch escaped death.

God extended his life right into eternity. Enoch provides a picture of eternal life, the gift we receive by faith.

He is more than a biblical type of eternal life, though. Enoch is the picture of a purposeful life. The rest of his story follows in Hebrews 11:6: "It's impossible to please God apart from faith. And why? Because anyone who wants to approach God must believe both that He exists and that He cares enough to respond to those who seek Him" *(The Message)*. Enoch's epitaph may not be inscribed in marble anywhere, but God tucked it away in Scripture instead. Enoch pleased God. I'd love an epitaph like that. I don't expect to escape death like Enoch did, but I'd like to experience life like he did. Enoch's life mattered.

Scripture paints a sketchy picture of his life. We don't have a collection of his spiritual journals revealing the secret of an amazing life, and he didn't author a best-selling book about his personal relationship with God. We're left instead with scraps of his existence. Twice in Scripture, Enoch's name enters a genealogy, he prophesies in the New Testament book of Jude, and he appears among the faithful of Hebrews 11. While we don't know many details about his life, we get the idea that the details aren't important. What matters is that Enoch pleased God during his time on earth. He entered eternity with his hands full of a life that counted.

Enoch first appears in Genesis 5, but the significance of his story goes back to the beginning. The beginning started with a bang. The Genesis 1 explosion of light resonated through the abysmal arms of space. God's voice sent light streaming across the darkness, erasing the black of eternity past. The universe sparkled with perfection. Then within the twinkle of a far-away star, a dingy film tainted its beauty. The scum of sin collected on God's handiwork, the light grew faint, and darkness reigned again. From Eden to Egypt, Genesis strains under the weight of an evil shroud. The beautiful beginnings fade into chapter after chapter of ugly humanity.

Born into an uneasy existence,
we are plagued by the question,
"Is this all there is?"

Nestled among stories of murder, rebellion, and immorality are two chapters of genealogies, the "sleeper sections" of Scripture. The pre-Flood genealogy of Genesis chapter 5 traces the descendants of Adam to Noah, while Genesis chapter 10 names the post-Flood generations of Noah. A casual reader who manages to stay awake through the lists of unfamiliar (and unpronounceable) names views them as historical filler to be skimmed or skipped. But God intended more for us than boredom when He recorded the generations of earliest mankind.

It's no coincidence that God placed the first genealogy right after the death of Abel, the first human to die. Although still new to the human race, death didn't need any practice. It entered the race sprinting and overtook the next six generations of contestants without pausing for breath. With staccato-like precision, the Bible's first genealogy pounds out the fates of men: Adam lived, became a father, and died. Seth lived, became a father, and died. Enosh lived, became a father, and died. Kenan lived, became a father, and died. Mahalalel lived, became a father, and died. Jared lived, became a father, and died. Scripture summarizes the long life of each man with shocking brevity. Into a single statement, 5,514 years of combined living are seemingly squeezed: they lived, had children, and died.

Like a dull headache swelling into a throbbing migraine, the genealogy is a crescendo of futility. The disturbing question of life emerges from the casualties of Genesis 5, and it has haunted every descendant of Adam since. We live, die, and pass the hollow baton to the next generation. Born into an uneasy existence, we are plagued by the question, "Is this all there is?"

God interrupts the listing of dead men to answer that question. In the seventh generation after Adam, God shouts "No!" through the life of Enoch, a seemingly ordinary man. He didn't slay giants, build arks, or conquer nations. He's seldom the topic of sermons and Sunday school lessons, because we don't really know much about him. He lived, had children, and disappeared.

In the repetitive account of ancients, Enoch breaks the monotony. He disrupts the pattern of life, fatherhood, and death in the generations from Adam to Noah.

> When Enoch had lived 65 years, he became the father of Methuselah. And after he became the father of Methuselah, Enoch walked with God 300 years and had other sons and daughters. Altogether, Enoch lived 365 years. Enoch walked with God; then he was no more, because God took him away.
>
> —Genesis 5:21–24

Walking with God

Enoch wasn't the first person to walk with God. On the sixth day of creation, God created His soul mate. He fashioned the human heart after His own, and He molded the human spirit into the shape of His own passions. After He'd sculpted the perfect image-bearer, He breathed His very life into its nostrils and "man became a living being" (Gen. 2:7). God poured Himself into a clump of dirt and transformed it into the one created thing that could connect with Him. For an undisclosed amount of time, Creator and created enjoyed each other. They walked together on the lush grasses of the Garden.

Then came the serpent and the seed of doubt: maybe God *was* withholding something even more wonderful than the walks in the cool mist of Eden evenings. When Adam tore into the forbidden fruit, he ripped apart more than the tender skin. He ripped apart a relationship; he ripped apart *the* relationship for which he was created. Before Adam even swallowed his mouthful of fruit, sin sucked the breath of life out of him. His heart no longer pumped God-rich blood; his spirit no longer sought God's pleasure. Separated from his soul mate and deprived of God's breath, he stumbled through life gasping for significance and searching for relationships. Evicted from his home, Adam limped alone across a desert strewn with brambles of confusion and pain.

We're still hobbling over those well-traveled paths, and the brambles haven't blown aside yet, but comparatively speaking, we've got it pretty easy today. God has revealed Himself to us through Scripture and the Incarnation, neither of which intersected the world of Genesis. It's no wonder that over half of Hebrews 11 applauds the faith of Genesis journeymen, who had so little to see and so little to believe.

In spite of the shadows, Enoch reached through the dark, found the firm hand of God, and didn't let go for three hundred years. Enoch connected with God and rediscovered Eden's soft grass. He found the God who wanted to be his

Friend. He found the God who longed to be known and loved by him. Enoch replaced the restless wandering of Cain and the futile living of his contemporaries with the steady walk of faith. By faith, he lived and *didn't* die to show us that there's more to life than birth, death, and the plethora of events in between. By faith, Enoch earned the epitaph of one who pleased God.

God-Pleasing Faith

Pleasing God, according to Hebrews 11:6, requires faith. Over 90 percent of Americans claim faith in God, but I'm quite sure that if God were to modernize the ancient chapter of faith, it wouldn't grow into a voluminous library. In our culture of convenience and comfort, *faith* is like the word *love;* it's a profound word we've simplified to the point of ineffectiveness. I love tacos, my country, and the color blue. I use the same word to describe my affinity for chocolate and my unbreakable bond to my mom. Tossing the word around as if it has a thousand replacements has lessened its significance. Through shallow usage, we've also dulled the point of the word *faith*. I have faith in the weatherman when I leave home without my umbrella. I have faith in my car mechanic when I drive out of the service lot. And, like 90 percent of Americans, I have faith in God when the pollsters ask. One simple word simultaneously captures whimsical wishes about the weather and a perfunctory belief in a Supreme Being.

God doesn't just ask the question;
He examines the life.

George Gallup Jr. didn't define faith in his survey. He merely asked a question: "Do you believe in God or a universal spirit?" An indifferent shrug or an easy nod answers the question. However, God doesn't just ask the question; He examines the life. The daily lives of ancient God-pleasers revolved around an immovable confidence in the Person and plan of God Almighty. They didn't sway or drift in the hurricanes of hard times. They believed what couldn't be seen; they held on to what couldn't be proven. When their circumstances shook with uncertainty, they were certain. When everyone else saw darkness, they walked in the light of God's presence. The God-pleasing faith of Enoch and his teammates of Hebrews 11 is a rarity, bordering on extinction in the masses of modern people who profess faith in God.

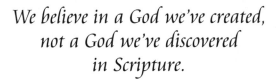

*We believe in a God we've created,
not a God we've discovered
in Scripture.*

God-pleasing faith is better explained in the latter part of Hebrews 11:6. "It's impossible to please God apart from faith. And why? Because anyone who wants to approach God must believe *both* that He exists *and* that He cares enough to respond to those who seek Him" (*The Message,* emphasis mine). There are two conditions to Enoch's kind of faith: first, believing God exists, and second, believing He cares enough to respond to those who seek Him.

He exists. I believe that *He,* the God of Scripture, exists. Faith does not begin with a general belief in some Supreme

Being; it sprouts from a *correct* concept of God. While research suggests that the United States is one of the most religious countries on earth, we believe in the wrong God. We believe in a God we've created, not the God revealed in Scripture. We've superimposed our concepts of sin, justice, love, and mercy on the reality of His revelation. We are, according to Gallup, a nation of biblical illiterates: "The stark fact is most Americans don't know what they believe or why."[1] We don't have a clue who God is or what He's really about.

He cares enough to respond. God is not a disinterested deity who sovereignly controls human events from a distance. He is a God of love who is intricately involved in human life. While salvation is His most celebrated involvement, redemption is just the door to endless gifts from the hand of God. God cares about my eternal destiny, but He also cares about my earthly journey. He cares about *me*. My small concerns may be dismissed by other friends, but they captivate Him. My repeated failures may frustrate other friends, but they fill Him with compassion. He was there before anyone else came, and He'll be there when everyone else has left.

A "Just Say the Word" Friend

Faith is believing that God is a "just say the word" kind of friend. I've got hundreds of acquaintances and dozens of friends, but my "just say the word" friends are an elite group. They are the ones who love me enough to do whatever I need. A "just say the word" friend brings me chicken soup and a sappy movie when I'm sick. A "just say the word" friend accompanies me on a retreat when I'm in charge, but neither of us wants to go. A "just say the word" friend drops everything to hitch up his trailer and help me move furniture. A "just say the word" friend is someone who knows my ugliness as well as my beauty and loves me for both. "Just say the word" friends give and give and give, just because they love me.

"Just say the word" friendships aren't accidents. They are gems mined after hours in the shafts of daily life. They are gold refined from time spent together in the fire. They are jewels polished by the rough edges of adversity. Time, heat, and pressure transform ordinary friendships into those of inestimable worth. Once I've recognized such a friendship, the pursuit begins. I devote myself to extracting the wealth locked inside the other person. I diligently seek knowing my friend.

God is not a cosmic acquaintance or a casual friend. From the beginning of time, He has revealed Himself as a "just say the word" friend, a rare value in a cheapened world. He sacrificed to restore a severed relationship, and He offers His friendship to the diligent seekers. He extends His hand to those like Enoch who, by faith, will grab it. He rewards those with Enoch's genuine faith—believing who God is and what He offers. That kind of faith is God-pleasing faith, and it generates commitment. "Commit" comes from a Latin word meaning "to connect," and by faith, Enoch connected with God. Genesis puts it another way: "Enoch walked with God."

A Grammar Lesson

Walking is my kind of exercise. That is, it's my kind of exercise *if* I'm going to exercise. To my doctor's consternation, exercise is a matter of convenience instead of commitment for me. I'm not really proud of this fact, but it is the way things are in my life right now. If the weather is nice and I've got some free time, I'll take a walk through the neighboring subdivision. Exercise can also be a pragmatic activity for me; if my jeans are tight, I'll find time to go walking a couple times a week. Sunshine and cellulite motivate me. I don't pretend to be a serious walker. "Walk" is more of a noun in my life; it's a hobby I have. I go for walks. My doctor would say "walk" should be a verb; it should be something I do. He'd like me to say, "I walk regularly." He's not impressed when I say "I go for a walk sometimes."

My friend Jason is a weight lifter. He's got a bug for body building. With unbroken resolve, he trots to the college gym six nights a week for an hour-long session with the weights. It's a hefty commitment of time and energy. His buddies, envious of his enormous biceps, vow to join him in the weight room. So they come. And they go. Within days, their body building careers are over, because they are not interested in the requirements for bulging muscles. They may dabble in lifting, but Jason lifts. Lift is a noun in their vocabulary; in Jason's, it's a verb.

Walking with God isn't so much about problems as it is about a Person.

My friend Glen is a runner. Dark mornings don't deter him. Rainy days don't ruin his resolve. Cold weather doesn't keep him in. Every morning, Glen leaves his cozy bed and subjects his tired body to a jarring five-mile jog. He sets goals and pushes himself to reach them. Every so often, my roommate, Tammy, likes to go jogging. She relieves stress, works up a sweat, and comes home refreshed. She's not fanatical about it. If the mood strikes, she goes. Tammy goes for an occasional run. Glen runs. For Tammy, run is a noun, but for Glen it's a verb.

If I believe that He exists and that His existence makes a difference in my life, I will wholeheartedly commit myself to Him. He is a Person to be loved, not a project to be tackled.

Jason's friends, Tammy, and I all have something in common besides our propensity for nouns and our aversion to verbs. We'd rather wish for rippling muscles, marathon finishes, and baggy blue jeans than sacrifice the sweat to get them. We'd rather envy the successes of our disciplined friends than endure aching muscles of our own. We'd rather choose the couch than the "ouch." Lifting, running, and walking are fun hobbies to pick up and set down again, but they aren't influential factors in our daily lives. We just aren't that committed.

Physically speaking, my lack of commitment is unhealthy. Spiritually speaking, such a lack of commitment would be utterly tragic. God has invited me to walk next to Him for life. He wants to reestablish the connection that was severed so long ago, and He sacrificed His Son to do it. When He reached through the dark to find me, I humbly took His hand and stepped onto the soft grass. I didn't realize then that I had embarked on the most incredible journey imaginable. I also didn't realize how much work it would be to stay next to Him, instead of stepping off the path into familiar territory.

From the barren stretches of sin, it's easy to talk about my walk with God instead of actually walking with Him. Merely having a walk with God allows space for convenience and comfort. It creates a hobby to be picked up or a project to be undertaken. If I happen to move away from Him, I talk about needing to pray longer, read more, get up earlier. I look for activities to fix the problem. Walking with God, though, isn't so much about problems as it is about a Person. The husband who says, "I want to work on my marriage," has the right idea, but the wrong focus. A marriage isn't a thing to be fixed; it's a person to be loved. The husband who says, "I really want to love my wife," understands that the person with whom he's spending life deserves his best attention and primary focus.

Becoming a Diligent Seeker

In spheres of singles, commitment is a word that's often avoided instead of embraced. Because I've not made a commitment to a certain person for life, it's easy to omit the word from my vocabulary. I'm spoiled by the "no strings attached" living. I'm used to coming and going according to my own schedule, and I like holding exclusive rights to my paycheck. However, marital status doesn't matter when it comes to following Christ. Like every other believer, I'm without excuse in the arena of commitment. The most amazing Person has already committed Himself to me for the here and the hereafter. If I believe that He exists and that His existence makes a difference in my life, I will wholeheartedly commit myself to Him. He is a Person to be loved, not a project to be tackled. He is the Person who deserves my best attention and primary focus. I will begin a journey that requires deep commitment. I will be a diligent seeker.

Diligent seeking isn't glamorous, but the rewards are unbeatable. I've experienced some seasons of deep commitment, and in the midst of them, I've known that there's nothing on earth like walking with God. A committed walker discovers territory unknown to the Christian couch potato or to the Christian "train riders."

As an adult, I made my first trip to Disney World. My Florida friends and I purchased tickets to do the montage of parks in a marathon week. On our day in the Magic Kingdom, we took the train tour to get a sweeping view of the grounds. The ride was nice, the scenery was great, and the breeze was refreshing, but the whole trip was highly unsatisfying. I watched others enjoy the surroundings, but from my bench on the train I missed all the delights of a park packed with opportunities. If I had stayed on the train, I would have missed the Magic Kingdom.

I'm glad to tell you that I didn't spend a small fortune to merely ride a comfortable train. I walked and walked and walked, deep into the heart of Walt's wonderland. I sweat mercilessly in winding lines of humanity; I clenched my fists on roller coasters; I hunted for souvenirs in a forest of shops; I licked greasy chicken off my fingers; and I giggled ridiculously at life-sized versions of animated favorites. It was a day of inexhaustible delight.

To assist their guests, Disney uses special names to mark off park territories. Each name indicates the kind of experiences a guest will encounter. For example, in Liberty Square, I visited the Hall of Presidents and took a ride on the riverboat. In Fantasyland, I met Snow White and ran for cover from an afternoon downburst to King Stefan's castle. In New Tomorrowland, I screamed in the dark of Space Mountain and hurried past the Alien Encounter. Each territory opened new doors of possibilities. From the train, I only saw the opportunities; on my feet, I indulged in them.

There are territories along the Christian journey that only walkers will fully experience. The marked-off regions elude those who only ride the train. The example of Enoch ushers us through four different realms of God's incredible kingdom on earth.

Happiness Hollow

Enoch's walk with God took him through Happiness Hollow, an amazing place where humans have the chance to make God smile. The words of Enoch's stunning epitaph can be mine, too. By my faith and commitment, I can please God.

When I was in grade school, I memorized a poem to please my dad. In our family poetry collection was the story of "Twenty Froggies," a poem he knew as a child. I'm not sure why he liked it so much, except it must have taken him back to a place that only existed in his memory. His eyes lit up when he recited parts to me. He grinned and chuckled at the sing-song rhyme of twenty frogs dressed in white vests going to school. Somewhere in the middle of one of his recitations, the wattage went off in my head: wouldn't he be excited if I learned his favorite poem, too?! I decided to memorize it and surprise him. With each learned phrase, I anticipated his glee. I worked hard to master every word, eager to present my poetic gift to my dad. I knew he would be delighted.

Delighting my dad pushed me past the minimum childhood requirement of obedience. I wasn't satisfied with just avoiding the wooden spoon. My relationship with my dad could be more than that. I knew I could make him beam, bust his buttons, and bless the day I was born. I would've gone to the moon to make him smile. Pleasing my dad was a mission of love—because I loved him, I poured my energy into making him glad to be my dad.

God is never satisfied to just save us, and it's not enough that we try to obey Him.

Having an earthly dad that I admire and respect has always been my great privilege. Being able to please him with wholehearted love has been an even greater privilege. Neither compare, though, to having a heavenly Dad. I would be thrilled if I could simply pacify the anger of a holy God through strict adherence to His divine rules. It's incomprehensible that I can make a smile break across the face of Almighty God. My fragile faith somehow gives Him glee. I don't have to dodge lightning bolts; instead I can pour my energy into delighting my Dad. I can please God.

Friendship Field

Enoch also traveled across Friendship Field on his earthly journey. While he knew and pleased God as his father, he also knew Him as a friend. God is never satisfied to just save us, and it's not enough that we try to obey Him. Remember the reason He came? He came to restore what was lost in Eden. God's plan all along has been to put the pieces of a broken *friendship* back together.

Growing up, I believed that the sum total of my dad's existence was that he was my dad. That was his job. Whatever he went away to do all day was insignificant. Whatever the stacks of paper on his desk were for didn't matter. He was my dad. He didn't do anything else important.

As I grew older, though, I began to realize that my dad was a real person. He had his own life and history that were just as real as the ones I was making. He had thoughts and perspectives and hurts that I could not have understood in my immaturity. It wasn't until I had lived enough of my own life that I began to appreciate his, and I realized that our relationship didn't have to be limited to dad and daughter. We had life in common. We could be friends.

God is like that. When I diligently seek Him, I find more than my heavenly Father; I find my Eternal Friend. For a lifetime, I get to cultivate a friendship that will culminate in eternity. As I daily peer into the kaleidoscope of His Person and glimpse His dazzling beauty, I am unfailingly awestruck. He sets gift upon gift in front of me, the diligent seeker. Each gift leads to another in Friendship Field. Just like Him, they never end. Every day He invites me deeper into His heart. This is a search with a guarantee. Seekers *will* find Him; He *will* reward those who diligently seek Him.

Purpose Park

Just beyond Friendship Field is Purpose Park, an enclosed arena that offers a rewarding existence to those inside. Winding lines of harried people wait outside, willing to pay astronomical amounts to pass through the gates. Some have already purchased tickets from fraudulent entrepreneurs. A father sacrificed his son's baseball season to earn a promotion; a businessman offered his integrity to fill a need while out of town; a secretary gave up her paycheck to buy synthetic self-esteem from the department store racks. Waving their tickets, they search for a gate that will admit them to the park. Like most of the people around them, they ignore the occasional murmur that says the Owner of the park has already bought their tickets. While they roll their eyes at the ridiculous rumor, they don't see those who leave the lines, meet the Owner, and walk into the Park at His side.

The longer I walk with God, the less I care about how things work out for me, and the more I care about how much like Jesus I look.

Enoch spent the last three hundred years of his life inside Purpose Park. He was just an ordinary guy who flashed in and out of history like a shooting star. He's a blip in the Genesis genealogy, living nearly a third less time on earth than any of his contemporaries. He got everything out of life that they did; he lived, had children, and passed on his heritage. That is, Enoch got everything they got out of life except the empty search for purpose. His life was not a collection of scattered circumstances; each event, each choice, each moment was a stitch in the handiwork of God.

A familiar illustration compares life to a piece of needlework that God sees from the top, while I can only see the messy underneath. He knows what stitches are needed to complete the picture, and only He sees how they all work together. I don't usually understand how the mess creates something of beauty. I do know, however, what picture God is making. God is weaving my life into the likeness of Jesus. Every prick of the needle, every break of the thread has a purpose; it's a stitch of Jesus. The longer I walk with God, the less I care about how things work out for me, and the more I care about how much like Jesus I look.

I love living in Purpose Park. It's a place of peace where I never have to worry about futility. Everything I do counts, because it's all threaded through God's needle.

Mystery Mountain

"They looked all over and couldn't find him because God had taken him" (Heb. 11:5, *The Message*). When Enoch walked off the earth after three hundred years of keeping in step with God, he apparently didn't leave a forwarding address. The search party found no trace of him. He simply vanished. Likely, the legend of Enoch furnished stories for generations of children after him. It's quite possible that no one knew what happened to Enoch until God wrote the story centuries later. Enoch left the world mystified. His walk with God on and off the earth took him into territory they couldn't understand.

There's nothing on earth like walking with God because there's no one on earth like God.

A close walk with God baffles onlookers. They see radiance that defies description. They observe peace that eludes understanding. They witness passion that surpasses human devotion. They see strength that violates common sense. They see God, but they don't recognize Him. His life breathed into humanity the first time was a mystery; it brought dust to life. His life breathed into humanity the second time is a greater mystery; it brings death to life. It makes no sense, but it's true.

I almost love the sketchy story of Enoch more than the familiar tales of David or Moses. I won't be chosen to lead a nation into battle or out of slavery. My life will be nondescript in comparison to theirs, and my mark on the world will seem small. However, there's nothing to keep me from living like Enoch. He's not a hero of the faith because he did big things for God. He's a hero of the faith because he did the little things *with* God every day. He committed himself to walking with God.

There's nothing on earth like walking with God because there's no one on earth like God. He created me to be with Him, and when I follow the tug of my heart I taste the unrivaled thrill of discovering Him. He does reward those who seek Him, and while the rewards are many, the greatest one is God Himself. If I seek Him, I will find Him and forever enjoy the feast of His friendship.

The genealogy in Genesis 5 doesn't end with Enoch. The drumbeat of doom resumes its rhythm after God took him away. Methuselah lived, became a father, and died. Lamech lived, became a father, and died. The genealogy needs Enoch. He's tucked in there to remind us that the trip from the womb to the tomb doesn't have to be meaningless. There's something that makes the whole thing count.

9

Amram and Jochebed:
Living Beyond Fear

*It's not for sissies, you know . . . dining alone. You gotta
be made of some pretty stern stuff to do that. See the
trick is to seem mysterious, like the choice is yours.*

—Justine Matisse, *Hope Floats*

When Franklin Delano Roosevelt took office in 1933,
he faced the daunting job of putting a crumbling nation
back together. Three years of the deepening Depression had
decimated the economy and destroyed the American dream.
In his first inaugural address, Roosevelt spoke words to ig-
nite a flicker of hope. "The only thing we have to fear is
fear itself," he boomed across the airwaves.

He was wrong. While his rallying cry generated confidence
over the following months, even a resurrected national mo-

rale couldn't change reality. Workers still lost jobs, families still starved, banks still failed, businesses still closed. Valid causes of fear waited at every turn, just like they do today. A catastrophe is always at bat, on deck, and in the dugout.

The rules may have changed outside the Garden, but the Ruler did not.

It's not the way God made the world. Adam and Eve never gave a thought to their safety in the garden paradise because it wasn't necessary. God was in control, and the world was perfect. When they ate the forbidden fruit, though, they sacrificed that security. In an instant, everything seemed to change. Satan's grip closed around the globe, and sin took root in their souls. Adam and Eve spiraled into a world of frightening uncertainty, groping for control when everything seemed out of control.

Fear is all about control. When I think I am in control, I am not afraid. When someone I trust is in control, I am not afraid. Fear takes over when no one, or the wrong person, takes charge. Given these limitations, I have much to fear! My power is minuscule, and trustworthy people can only carry their influence so far. Evil lurks everywhere.

The paradox of the Fall, though, is that while the world often succumbs to the efforts of Satan and the effects of sin, God is still in control. The rules may have changed outside the Garden, but the Ruler did not. Instead of living at peace under His sovereign hand, however, I cower in corners and quiver at what is unknown to me. God longs to lure me out of those corners into His confidence, and He does it through the example of those who lived without fear in the midst of the most dreadful circumstances.

A Reign of Terror

By faith Moses' parents hid him for three months after he was born, because they saw he was no ordinary child, and they were not afraid of the king's edict.

—Hebrews 11:23

During the reign of an unnamed Pharaoh, baby showers in Goshen, Egypt, were monochromatic. "Think Pink" was always the theme. No blue streamers hung from the sun-baked brick; no blue frosting coated the cupcakes. Neighbors prayed pink blessings on expectant Hebrew mothers. Sons, the pride of a patriarchal culture, were dreaded. Sons, the strength of God's chosen people, brought sentences of death.

It hadn't always been like that. Four hundred years earlier, the Israelites entered Egypt as the esteemed family of Joseph, vice president of the wealthiest and most powerful country in the world. Driven by hunger, the seventy chosen people of God left the Promised Land and applied for residence visas in far-away Egypt where food was plentiful. Pharaoh, friend of Joseph, invited them to settle in Goshen and even employed the best among them to work in his stables. With food on the table and family across the street, life was good for the Hebrew people.

Life was good for the moment, but dark clouds gathered in the prophetic distance, casting a shadow across future generations. Generations earlier, God had promised Abraham a son, a nation, and a homeland, but He had also forecast turbulent weather. Genesis 15:13–16 records the impending storm: "The LORD said to him, 'Know for certain that your descendants will be strangers in a country not their own, and they will be enslaved and mistreated four hundred years. But I will punish the nation they serve as slaves, and afterward they will come out with great possessions. . . . In the fourth generation your descendants will come back here." If Abraham had told his descendants the whole story of God's promise, and it's likely that he did, then the Israelites knew their time in Egypt wouldn't be a Mediterranean vacation. They also knew that it would be a long time before they returned "home."

During those years, God fulfilled the second part of His promise to Abraham. A nation was born. Literally. Rabbits appeared infertile compared to the reproductive skills of the Israelite captives. The Bible begins describing the baby boom by saying the people "were fruitful and increased greatly in number" (Gen. 47:27). By Exodus chapter 1, they "were fruitful and multiplied greatly and became exceedingly numerous, so that the land was filled with them" (v. 7). Seventy Israelites swelled into thousands, and when Pharaoh looked up from a palace game of senet, he got scared. A separate nation of people was living under his proud nose, and he feared a revolt. Under the guise of "dealing shrewdly" with them, he initiated a political plan to weaken them. He revoked their passports and made them captives in his country. The Israelites became Pharaoh's enslaved labor force, and he assigned ruthless slave masters to make their lives miserable.

The slave masters excelled at their assignment, but Pharaoh's plan backfired anyway. Instead of diminishing the Hebrew population, the oppression actually increased the number of Israelites. "The more they were oppressed, the more they multiplied and spread" (v. 12).

When Plan A failed, Pharaoh turned to Plan B and the Hebrew midwives to suppress the prolific people. "When you help the Hebrew women in childbirth and observe them on the delivery stool," he ordered, "if it is a boy, kill him; but if it is a girl, let her live" (v. 16). Unlike the henchmen of Plan A, the Hebrew midwives feared God. They defied the king's orders and let the boys live. Again, instead of weakening the Jewish nation, Pharaoh had stumbled on another way to strengthen them: "So God was kind to the midwives and the people increased and became even more numerous" (v. 20).

The Israelite infestation alarmed Pharaoh, but his inability to curb their growth infuriated him. When his first two schemes flopped, he abandoned the covert activity and issued an order to all his people concerning the Jews: "Every boy that is born you must throw into the Nile, but let every girl live" (1:22). Plan C deputized an entire nation. Safe places and sympathetic people didn't exist for pregnant Hebrew women.

The edict thundered across the land, shattering dreams and shredding families. Fear replaced what should have been excitement in Hebrew birthing rooms as Pharaoh's forceps of death reached into unwilling wombs and emerged with possible prey. Mothers pushed through the pain of birth, but recoiled from the pronouncement of life. "It's a boy." The words sliced through the stifling Sahara air like a guillotine. When the screams should have been over, they were just beginning. "It's a boy." Cries of physical pain became heart-wrenching sobs of emotional anguish. Egyptian patriots snatched squalling baby boys from weeping Hebrew parents and whisked them from the nursery to the Nile.

The Nile River has always been the life of Egypt. For thousands of years, it has flowed across the scorching sands and deposited its rich sediment on Egyptian farmland. Without it, the country is a wasteland. Early in the book of Exodus, however, the overflowing waters of life became a raging current of death, swallowing the infant sons of a people in bondage. While crocodiles feasted on the precious flesh of God's tiniest chosen children, the scourge of slavery struck its hardest blow on the backs of a beaten people. The ancient promise of deliverance seemed to ebb away, swept out to sea with the memories of lost sons.

Perhaps God had forgotten them. They hadn't heard from Him in a long time, and life in Egypt had gotten progressively worse. Pharaoh had no limits to his brutality, and the Israelites didn't want to imagine what he might do next. Fear reigned on the throne of Pharaoh and gripped the hearts of the Hebrews.

A Refusal to Fear

On a dusty Goshen street lived a little family that didn't seem like anyone special. The quiet couple and their two small children blended in with dozens of other families. Years of slavery had scarred their bodies and seared their hearts, just like it had all their neighbors. Yet when this tired mother rocked her toddling son to sleep, she sang him songs of hope. When this weary father tucked in his young daughter, he whispered sweet words of freedom in her ear. Surrounded by the fear of insurmountable obstacles, they somehow clung to a promise spoken generations earlier and passed on to them. They believed the promise of their silent God.

As the birth of their third child approached, Amram and Jochebed must have trembled to think what was ahead. The Bible tells their story very simply, not even using their names until chapters later: "Now a man of the house of Levi married a Levite woman, and she became pregnant and gave birth to a son" (Exod. 2:1–2). Most Hebrew genealogies of the time would have continued "and he was taken by the authorities and thrown into the river according to the order of Pharaoh."

The story of baby Moses changes the plot. "When [Jochebed] saw that he was a fine child, she hid him for three months" (Exod. 2:2). Hebrews 11 restates and amplifies the story: "By faith Moses' parents hid him for three months after he was born, because they saw he was no ordinary child, and they were not afraid of the king's edict" (Heb. 11:23).

Faith overcame fear as Amram and Jochebed plunged themselves into danger on behalf of their infant son. Faith prompted a nondescript set of parents to take bold action, unknowingly preparing a nation for divine deliverance. According to the details of Hebrews 11:23, Amram and Jochebed lived out their rare faith for two reasons.

God Created the Opportunity

"They saw he was no ordinary child."

"Of all the babies I've ever seen, he's one of them." My dad's standard response to all newborns extended even to his own grandchildren. Coming home from the hospital hours after the birth of a new grandson, Grandpa had an extra bounce in his step and another twinkle in his green-flecked eyes. He was definitely in love with the tiny new person he'd just met, but he was not particularly impressed by his looks. When it comes to newborns he never is, and frankly, neither is most of the world. Newborns are notoriously unattractive. Most exit the birth canal wrinkled and red, with remarkable resemblance to the infant in the next crib. It usually takes a little time, sleep, and milk to transform a blotchy baby into cooing cuteness.

While most babies don't win beauty contests at birth, every newborn takes first place in the Wonders of the World competition. Nothing on the planet is as amazing as the exquisite perfection of a brand new little person. Silky skin, curled fingers, and fuzzy heads create an endearing masterpiece of miniature proportions. Every baby is extraordinary. It's the common denominator of all births. Length and ease of labors vary, size and shape of infants differ, but all parents think their baby makes the stars shine.

So why does God waste the words to say the obvious about baby Moses? Except for Jesus, Moses is the only major Bible character we encounter as an infant, and three different times Scripture records that Moses was an extraordinary baby.

> *When she saw that he was a fine child, she hid him for three months.*
>
> —Exodus 2:2

> *At that time, Moses was born, and he was no ordinary child. For three months he was cared for in his father's house.*
>
> —Acts 7:20

> *By faith Moses' parents hid him for three months after he was born, because they saw he was no ordinary child.*
>
> —Hebrews 11:23

Maybe he fit in the "non-wrinkled" category. Perhaps he had a tangle of dark hair instead of peach fuzz. Baby Moses was probably an agreeable baby with extraordinary good looks.

So what. Amram and Jochebed didn't risk their lives to save Moses just because he was a gorgeous baby. If he had been born with a face only a mother could love, she would have loved it and longed to save him. If he had been scrawny and screaming, his parents would not have happily tossed him into the Nile. It doesn't matter what a baby looks like; loving parents don't discard children based on appearance and temperament.

I am sure that all Hebrew parents in Egypt wanted to save their children. They didn't willingly sacrifice their children on the altar of Pharaoh's ego. If it had been possible, they would have saved their sons. However, Pharaoh was not only ruthless; he was effective. He managed to enforce his barbaric law, eliminating a generation of Hebrew boys.

Yet Moses escaped the insanity. He was not only extraordinary for his looks, but he was extraordinary because Pharaoh and his recruits didn't know he existed. The unwritten circumstances of his birth somehow made it possible for Amram and Jochebed to save him. Perhaps Jochebed's neighbors hadn't detected her pregnancy. Maybe Moses came quickly before anyone nearby knew what had happened. Whatever the circumstances, when Jochebed gave birth, she and Amram looked at Moses, looked around, and looked at each other. They knew they had a chance to save the baby. God controlled the circumstances, and they took a sphinx-sized step of faith.

The Bigness of God Shrunk Pharaoh Down to Size

"They were not afraid of the king's edict."

On a college missions trip to Santiago, Chile, I encountered fear. Our team of three girls stayed with Sandy and

Kathy, two short-term missionary teachers who spoke only scraps of Spanish. Sandy chauffeured our fivesome around Santiago in her unreliable car, Puff the Tragic Wagon. On a day off from school, we decided to expand our touristic horizons, so we piled into Puff and headed to the coastal city of Vina del Mar. Halfway to our destination, Puff started limping. We pulled off to the side of the desolate road, changed the tire, and continued on our way. Puff apparently felt the need to defend her reputation that day, so not far down the road, she started limping again. We pulled over only to discover that the spare tire didn't like its new assignment. We were stuck. Five English-speaking girls, a disabled vehicle, a Chilean countryside, and no cell phone created lots of problems and few solutions.

I was afraid. We were desperate. When a Spanish-speaking stranger pulled over, we cheered with a fair amount of fear. Since we were helpless without him, we took deep breaths, prayed hard, and climbed into his car. I tried not to think about where he was taking us or what my parents would say if they knew where I was. Catching the fearful eyes of my friends, I hoped with them that he was a Good Samaritan and not an ax murderer. We exhaled in silent relief when we reached a phone several miles down the road.

Sandy and Kathy vaguely remembered that there was a missionary man in Vina del Mar. After some mental gymnastics, they came up with a name, tracked down a phone number, and dialed in desperation. I'm sure Arnie Smith was a busy man with a full schedule, but he was also the father of daughters. It took him only an instant to hear the fear in our voices. He dropped everything and became our dad for the day. When the phone rested back in the receiver, it took my fear with it. Arnie Smith was bigger than our problem. He would take care of it.

Amram and Jochebed weren't stuck on the side of the road, but they were trapped in a murderous system. They didn't know when Pharaoh's soldiers might crash through their door. They couldn't be sure Moses wouldn't wail at midnight. The future held terrifying uncertainties, yet the humble couple were not afraid. They had dialed heaven and handed their predicament over to Someone who could deal with it. Cradled in their arms was the greatest demonstration of God's power and Person, a constant reminder that He was big enough to take care of it. Fear disappeared.

By faith, obstacles can become opportunities to do the right thing and invitations to see God.

The world is a scary place. Every age and stage of life has its unique sources of fear. When I was a child, after I saw the TV Waltons' house burn down, I was sure ours was next. Creaks in the hall came from burglars sneaking toward my bedroom. Pain in my leg meant cancer and inevitable amputation. Headaches could only be from a brain tumor. A late night or early morning phone call carried bad news. A stomachache signaled pregnancy (these fears disappeared after I learned the truth about the pregnancy process!). A delayed parent picking me up was certainly a fatal car crash.

Some of these fears evaporated with experience and knowledge, but others have persisted into adulthood. Phone calls during "off hours" still start the adrenaline rush. Recurring aches and pains still make me vacillate between calling the doctor or not. Expected arrival times gone awry still make me fear the worst. To these childhood fears, I've added a whole new set of adult fears. The health of my parents, the salvation of my relatives, the condition of the economy, the global threat of terrorism, and the rise of local violence all regularly attack my peace of mind.

Then in their own little category are the fears I credit to singleness. They are not knee-knocking, palm-sweating fears like some. Instead they usually persist as a dull dread in the pit of my stomach. I'm afraid of always being alone in a crowd of couples. I'm afraid of continued rejection by someone I want to meet at the end of the aisle. I'm afraid of turning down a really wonderful guy who thinks I paint the sunset. I'm afraid of doing my taxes, tending my car, and planning my retirement by myself. I'm afraid of close friends moving on or moving away, leaving me to replace them—again. In a sentence, I'm afraid I'll never get married.

Since the break-up between God and man in the Garden, fear has lived in the human heart and has ravaged the human mind. One of Satan's key weapons, fear distorts perspective and threatens contentment. The message of Moses's parents, however, is that fear doesn't have to take over my thoughts and control my actions. By faith, obstacles can become opportunities to do the right thing and invitations to see God.

Mining Diamonds from Coal

Carolers tell us that Christmas is the most wonderful time of the year. I'm not going to argue with them, but I'm going to add that it's also the craziest time of the year. Bundled in thermal layers while squeezing through driven crowds is not always so wonderful. The annual adventure of gift buying can push me to my financial and emotional limit. I do it, though, because it shows love and appreciation to significant people in my life, and because I wouldn't find anything under the tree with my name on it if I didn't.

Christmas gifts come in four categories: coal, underwear, chocolate, and diamonds. Coal gifts are the Chia Pets of Christmas. You're not sure what you did to deserve such a gift, but you hope you never do it again. Underwear gifts are exactly what they sound like. Socks, ties, and underwear appear on the endless list of things you need but would rather just find in your dresser instead of under the Christmas tree. Chocolate gifts comprise the majority of gifts; they are the small, fun gifts that don't cost a fortune but represent sweet thoughts of you. Diamond gifts are the unexpected treasures under the tree. They are expressions of lavish love that you never dreamed of asking for and never expected to receive.

My mom is the head shopper in our family, and since her children have all grown up, she's simplified the gift-buying process. Most of her purchases come directly from lists we submit for her convenience. At our requests, she buys a fair amount of underwear. Then she adds her own special chocolate touches to the piles of wrapped boxes. She's an expert at avoiding the coal aisles in local stores, and she tries to make annual purchases from the diamond counter.

God is the master gift giver. He is a loving parent who spends a lifetime giving good gifts to His children. Food in the refrigerator, gas in the car, and strength for the day are the "underwear" items we generally include on our submitted lists, and He provides. He regularly wraps up "chocolate" gifts for us, too—a kind card in a moment of discouragement, a monetary gift in a season of scarcity, a canceled activity in a day of fatigue. His specialty, though, is diamonds. Under the tree of Calvary lay His greatest diamond. In the Person of His Son, He extended the real "Hope Diamond," an offer of eternal life for hopeless humanity. That diamond outshines the sun, adding its sparkle to every dark corner of life, but God didn't stop there. Diamonds fall from His fingertips, showering His children with indescribable wealth. Faithful friends, fulfilling jobs, devoted spouses, and growing children may top the list of diamond gifts, but they can never exhaust it.

Singleness isn't coal or underwear
or even chocolate. It's a diamond.

The New Testament epistles reveal an array of God's diamond gifts, the spiritual gifts He gives to each believer. Christians form the body of Christ, a body with many members and functions, and God equips that body to accomplish His purposes. In His infinite wisdom, He gives a different package to each of us. Your package might include several gifts in generous proportions, while mine may only have one. It's not my job to judge the Giver; instead, I need to unwrap my gift and make the most of it for the glory of the Giver.

I used to browse the list of spiritual gifts, evaluating the ones I might have and hurrying past the ones I didn't want. Actually, I hurried past the *one* I didn't want. Singleness. As I skipped over it, I'd quickly mention to God that I really thought marriage was the gift He should give to me. Singleness was a better gift for someone else. Seems like God didn't listen to me. He gave me the gift I didn't want and withheld the one I did want. At this point in the story, Satan suggests that God put His best wrapping paper around a chunk of coal. Some days it's easy to believe that and curl my lip in distaste at His gift. Tugging at my heart, though, is the fact that God only gives good gifts to His children. Singleness isn't coal or underwear or even chocolate. It's a diamond. It's a gift He tenderly enclosed in my package because He knew it was the perfect gift for me. He wants me to be delighted, not disgruntled. He wants me to recognize the possibilities He's placed before me.

Using the Batteries Provided

The most disappointing words to an excited child on Christmas morning are "batteries not included." Receiving a gift and then not having the power to use it is frustrating. God, the loving Father of Christmas, never gives gifts to His children without including the batteries. He, in fact, is the battery. He provides the power for the satisfying use of His gifts. God is big, and His power is limitless. The world is full of dangers that disintegrate at His omnipotent touch. The God who parts the waters, raises the dead, feeds the multitudes, and heals the sick is not threatened by anything. He is not baffled about the problems that keep me awake at night, nor is He paralyzed by what scares me. God has the power to eliminate any source of fear from my life.

I believe this with all my heart, but I still struggle with fear. My faith in God's power doesn't automatically ease my fear because, although God is big enough to bail me out, He sometimes allows me to tread a significant amount of water in what appears to be a sinking ship. Even though I believe in His bigness, my fears may still become reality. My worst nightmares can still come true.

∾

Indeed God is big, but He doesn't always choose to manifest His strength in the way I want.

∾

On a sunny spring day, I witnessed somebody's worst nightmare come true. I watched a mother and father stand in front of the caskets holding the bodies of two sons. I lamely hugged an adolescent sibling and offered my inadequate condolences. I sniffled through a service that sought to bring meaning from seemingly senseless deaths. God was big enough to prevent the car accident that claimed the lives of the two teenagers on their way home from the grocery store. He was big enough to adjust the angle of impact and spare their lives. He didn't.

The following spring, I witnessed the same worst nightmare come true for another family. I hurt for the mother and father who stood in front of two caskets. I grieved for the child left behind to grow up without his brother and sister. I cried for the grandma who drove the car that spun out of control. God was powerful enough to swerve the semi that smashed into their car. He was big enough to cushion them from the blows that killed them. He didn't.

Indeed God is big, but He doesn't always choose to manifest His strength in the way I want. That, in fact, is an even greater part of His bigness. More amazing than His power to prevent tragedy is His ability to bring good out of bad, to salvage significance from sorrow. God's perspective on the world is very different from my own. I see the world myopically, only able to focus on what concerns me and those close to me. His eyes, however, see everything. He sees what I don't. He knows what is best, and He's big enough to accomplish it.

Amram and Jochebed recognized the opportunity placed before them, and they believed in a big God. They did what they could, refused to be intimidated, and left the rest to Him. That's all any faithful follower can do. God may not guarantee happy endings this side of heaven, but He does promise to make a way through the darkest nights and the deepest waters.

Whenever life threatens me, I can be afraid, or I can choose to trust. Fear comes naturally. I see my whole life in one glimpse and think I have to solve all the issues. I want answers for the unknowns and solutions for the problems. The scary parts loom over me, and I struggle for control. I fight to get what I want, but somehow I end up losing more than I gain. I lose peace of mind and enjoyment of life. I waste time and opportunities. I forfeit the richness of life that God can still create on this fallen planet.

Fear is a lump in my throat, rising without effort. Trust is the constant swallowing of truth, sending the lump back to its place. Truth: God only gives good gifts. Truth: God is still in control. With each swallow, my tightly squeezed eyes open to see diamonds where I thought there was only coal. With each swallow, my trembling hands relax in the omnipotent grip of my big God. With each swallow, my pounding heart slows in the calming presence of the One who's in control.

"The LORD is my light and my salvation—whom shall I fear? The LORD is the stronghold of my life—of whom shall I be afraid?" (Ps. 27:1). The only thing to fear is not fear itself, as FDR asserted, but life without the God who's big enough to be in control.

10

Saul, Esau, and Solomon: Living Without Distraction

Therefore, since we are surrounded by such a great cloud of witnesses, let us throw off everything that hinders and the sin that so easily entangles, and let us run with perseverance the race marked out for us. Let us fix our eyes on Jesus, the author and perfecter of our faith, who for the joy set before Him endured the cross, scorning its shame, and sat down at the right hand of the throne of God.

—Hebrews 12:1–2

*A*part from recess and gym, lunch is the best part of the school day for most students. I always enjoyed the break from classes and the time with friends, but most days I didn't long for lunch strictly on the merits of my brown bag. My lunch was exceedingly predictable: a sandwich (bologna and cheese for years), a piece of fruit, two cookies, and a thermos of milk. I never did very well at the lunch table market—would you have traded your bag of Doritos or a Hostess Twinkie for my apple? Neither would my classmates.

I understand why the mother of four children and one paycheck made lunches the way she did. However, when I pack my own lunch these days, I do it a little differently. First, I start with a plastic grocery bag instead of the traditional brown lunch bag. Then I open the refrigerator and begin the search. If I want a salad, I grab the bag of lettuce, the package of cheese, the bunch of carrots, and the bottle of dressing. On a really good day, I'll find a stalk of broccoli and maybe a green pepper. Then from the pantry, I add the box of croutons and the canister of bacon bits to my growing feast. I also include a container of yogurt, an apple, and maybe some leftovers from a recent meal at Mom's. If I'm packing cookies, two is the number I eat *while* I'm packing the bagful.

A huge salad and leftovers make a satisfying lunch, but on a *really* good day, the gourmet treat in the bag is a sandwich. When I make a sandwich, I smear mayonnaise on a big butter-top roll. Then I stuff the bun with layers of shredded honey-roasted turkey, a juicy slice of tomato, thick slabs of cheddar cheese, half a dozen hamburger pickles, and several leaves of crispy lettuce. (Most mornings I can't wait until lunch to eat such a good sandwich, and it becomes my midmorning snack instead!)

The fastest way to ruin a good sandwich is to yank out the bottom half of the bun. With its innards splattered across the table, the sandwich is no longer a sandwich. It's just a mess. Another way to ruin a sandwich is to remove the top half of the bun, condemning the sandwich to a slow death. The pickles will slide off, the tomato can't stay in place, and the cheese falls out. The top of the bun keeps everything in its right place. The sandwich may still have the right ingredients, but it's arranged all wrong, and it has trouble staying together. Eventually it will fall apart.

Don't Forget the Lettuce

There's a sandwich in Hebrews 12. It's not made with a thick roll and honey-roasted turkey, though. It's strictly a lettuce sandwich, or actually, it's a "let us" sandwich. Three "let us" admonitions appear in the first two verses: "*Let us* throw off everything that hinders and the sin that so easily entangles, and *let us* run with perseverance the race marked out for us. *Let us* fix our eyes on Jesus" (vv. 1–2, emphasis mine).

For eight chapters, we've worn the sandals of Old Testament heroes who ran their races with perseverance. We've stepped in the ancient footsteps of their faithfulness. We've layered their examples into a sandwich that will take a lifetime to digest. Encasing the faithful examples are two critical qualifications for completing the sandwich—the bun, if you will. The bottom bun, the foundation of the sandwich, is a warning against entangling sins and hindrances. If the warning is ignored, the bun is yanked out and the sandwich destroyed. The top bun, then, is the summarizing challenge to fix our eyes on Jesus. If that bun is kept in place, every part of the sandwich stays properly aligned.

I've been part of singles groups long enough to make two observations: *everyone* changes and *everything* stays the same. In a twenties class especially, the turnover rate of members is out of this world. Between majors and marriages, colleges and careers, everyone seems to be going somewhere.

Regardless of who comes and goes, though, the issues and problems affecting young singles don't change. They may come disguised in different clothing with different music sounding in their ears, but no one is fooled. The questions are always the same: What am I going to do with my life? Whom will I marry? Why doesn't anyone like me? Do I fit in anywhere? Will I be successful? Will I like the career I've chosen?

In addition to these ongoing questions, I've also observed three persistent problems that infect singles groups. Two of them are "bottom bun yankers"—sins that destroy lives, and handicaps that send runners to the sidelines faster than anything else. The other problem is a top bun issue, a lack of focus that won't instantly ruin a life, but will keep the runner limping until he finally steps to the side.

Four thousand years of Old Testament history may have produced only one New Testament chapter of faithful followers, but they leave dozens of examples *not* to emulate. Three in particular seem to personify the three problems that often plague singles. Saul, the first king of Israel, struggled with and was defeated by the Siamese twin sins of bitterness and envy. Esau, twin brother of patriarch Jacob, spent his life on the sidelines because he settled for temporary satisfaction. Unlike Saul and Esau, Solomon accomplished great things for God in his life, but he did it without the top bun. His life slowly fell apart because he failed to fix his eyes on what mattered most. Saul, Esau, and Solomon are three very different men with one very important thing in common: they do not appear in Hebrews 11. Whatever else they did or didn't do in their lives, their lasting legacy is that they were not faithful. They did not receive a "well done, good and faithful servant" at the finish line.

Saul—Bitterness and Envy, the Siamese Twin Sins

When God chose Saul to be the first king of Israel, everything looked good. His initial appearance in 1 Samuel 9–10 reveals a humble, funny, well-mannered, one-of-a-kind candidate for the kingship. God doesn't label someone as an "impressive young man without equal among the Israelites" for nothing (9:2). Saul was tall, dark, handsome, and oozed leadership potential. (Sounds like the kind of guy all my single girlfriends are looking for!) What began as a promising career as king of Israel, however, ended in misery and destruction. He rapidly became a malicious monster who hurled spears at his servant and his son, and eventually hurled himself on his own spear.

The problems started in a town called Gilgal, where King Saul was to wait seven days for Prophet Samuel to meet him so they could offer sacrifices to the Lord. Days prior to the meeting, the Israelite army had attacked a Philistine outpost near Gilgal, antagonizing their Old Testament nemesis. While the Philistines gathered reinforcements and prepared to launch an intensive counterattack, Saul's terrified soldiers began to scatter. The seven days passed without a sign of Samuel, and the situation escalated into desperation. Saul made an executive decision in the interest of national security. He offered the sacrifices without Samuel.

The smoke was still rising from the altar when Samuel finally arrived. The prophet immediately asked, "What have you done?" and without a flinch Saul outlined his actions. Point number one: he was losing men. Point number two: Samuel was late. Point number three: the Philistines were preparing to attack. "So I felt compelled to offer the burnt offering," he concluded (13:12).

Samuel was not impressed. God's commands about sac-rifices were very clear, and Saul had ignored them. With-out a moment's consideration, Samuel pronounced God's displeasure saying, "You acted foolishly." Saul's simple de-cision would cost him the kingship, and changed him from a leader on the rise into a leader in demise.

Two of the most destructive forces among singles are bitterness and envy.

Pride prompted his initial decision, but it also kept him from repenting. Unable to humble himself before God, Saul became angry about where his life was going. He undoubt-edly had grand visions of a long and glorious reign, after which he would pass the scepter to his deserving son. When God dared to interrupt those plans and demand his com-pliance, Saul instead embarked on a lifestyle of bitterness and envy. He centered his career on the destruction of David, a faithful servant and soldier to whom God had promised the throne.

Let Him That Thinks He Stands . . .

Just about the time I start shaking my head at Saul's sin, God clubs me with the truth that's elusive to those involved (that would be me) but obvious to observers (that would be you): I share Saul's problem. (Thankfully, you do too.) My heart beats pride, and just like the fist-sized organ in my chest, it dictates nearly every step I take. I don't spend much time analyzing my circulatory system, and I just as easily leave pride out of my thinking. It's true that I don't really enjoy pondering my arrogance (it's pretty humbling), but sometimes pride is so subtle that it's easy to miss. I stand in a slow grocery line fuming about my valuable time. I rush a slow-moving student because I want to get to lunch. I want the bigger bedroom because, for some reason, my belongings deserve more space than my roommate's. I should be exempted from a mandatory meeting because I have important work to do. Every time I say, "I deserve something better than what I'm getting," pride pumps its debilitating venom through my life.

Sharing that heart of pride are the inseparable twin sins of bitterness and envy. Bitterness is the way I feel about *my* circumstances. Remember, I'm smart enough to know what's best for me, and when reality dares to disagree, I become angry. Anger leads quickly to bitterness about plans gone awry. If you've ever spat familiar phrases like, "What right does he have . . ." or "Who does she think . . ." or "It's not fair . . ." then you know what I'm talking about. Envy, on the other hand, is how I feel about *your* circumstances. When I look away from myself long enough to notice that a vicious twist of fate has given *you* what *I* deserve, envy consumes me.

Two of the most destructive forces among singles are bitterness and envy. I have a lot of single friends who, like me, didn't plan their lives the way they are happening. They pictured being passionately loved by an amazingly handsome man (my guy friends picture a stunningly beautiful woman), but instead they're pursued by those they'd rather leave for someone else (or worse yet, no one chases them at all). They expected that they would be liked and admired by all their peers, but instead they're clawing their way into a clique. They supposed they'd be surrounded by continuous good times, but instead they eat ice cream out of the carton on a quiet Friday night. These are not the things any of us planned on or prepared for, and when we entertain the thoughts that we deserve something better, we flirt with bitterness.

Then we look up from our unhappy circumstances and wonder why *she* isn't eating cookies and cream in her living room. We ask ourselves how *he* got invited to the party. We can't imagine what *he* sees in *her,* and while we stew over the unfairness of it all, envy comes alongside its twin.

⸻

God never promised fairness in our
fallen world, but my problem is that I think
I deserve it anyway.

⸻

Not only do we ruin our own relationship with God because of stubborn pride, but we also destroy our relationships with those around us. The writer of Hebrews calls it a bitter root that "grows up to cause trouble and defile many" (12:15). His contemporary, James, goes on to say "where you have envy and selfish ambition, there you find disorder and every evil practice" (3:16). That's a nice way of saying it. If I were to paraphrase James I would say, "where you have singles upset about their lives, you will find rumors, manipulation, cliques, division, and all kinds of Christian-coated nastiness."

Somehow we've missed the all-important lesson that fits into three simple words: life isn't fair. We proclaim it like it's a battle cry or a reason for God to change things—"Life's not fair!" Yup. We're right. It's not. Deal with it. God never promised fairness in our fallen world, but my problem is that I think I deserve it anyway. My real problem is that I don't want to let go of my pride and give in to God's plan. I don't want to admit that I'm cynical and ugly, and my bitterness and envy destroy me and the people around me.

Esau—Selling Out for Stew

It had been a long day for Suzy. My sister had mowed and trimmed the lawn, washed and waxed the car, and hoed and weeded the garden. When she finally collapsed at the kitchen table, I was just adding the finishing touches to a pot of hamburger stew, a family favorite.

"I'm starving!" she moaned. "Give me a bowl of that!"

"Sure," I said. "Just sign here first," I added, handing her a legal document.

"What's this?" she asked.

"Oh, it just says that for this bowl of stew you turn over to me all your rights to Mom and Dad's inheritance," I coolly replied.

"Pfff," she said, with a wave of her hand. "A lot of good an inheritance will do me if I die first from hunger! Give me the pen."

Yeah, right. And my sister owns East Asia if you want to buy part of it.

Only an absolute fool with utter disregard for value would make such a trade. People don't swap family inheritances for bowls of stew unless they are totally stupid.

Esau was totally stupid. After an exhausting day of work, he came home to Jacob's best smelling stew and signed away his future to get a bowl of it. He should have fixed himself something to eat, or he could have done what any other sibling would have done—yelled for Mom.

It's easy to see why Esau isn't among the faithful in

Hebrews 11; he wasn't even in the same race. His faithlessness shows itself clearly in three facts.

First, Esau was godless. Hebrews 12:16 makes this apparent: "see that no one is . . . godless like Esau, who for a single meal sold his inheritance rights as the oldest son." Godless simply means to be without God, to live as if He doesn't exist. Without God, Esau held the title for his life. He did whatever he wanted to do.

Secondly, Esau scorned value. As firstborn, he held a place of household authority and would inherit a double portion of his father's inheritance. The birthright was Esau's most valuable possession in terms of money and prestige, yet at the whiff of stew he tossed it aside and put his supper in its place.

Third, Esau was shortsighted. His stomach growled, and he filled it. The price tag didn't matter. We call this need to fulfill a desire *now* "instant gratification." All he saw was the bowl in front of his mouth. Esau couldn't step away from the table long enough to clear his vision. If he had, he would have realized that the stew was a temporary fix; he would be hungry again in a few hours. He would have realized that his birthright was a priceless possession that he could enjoy for a lifetime. Instead he sacrificed his future to momentarily fulfill a screaming desire.

Esau's hunger was legitimate. God created him to need food. However, he fulfilled that desire at a great cost. He traded what was extremely valuable for what would leave him hungry again.

Looking for Love in All the Wrong Places

My friend Anne understands Esau. An all-consuming hunger for love and happiness sent her to places she thought would satisfy. She left God out of her plans, assuming sole responsibility for gaining what she craved. Believing only marriage and motherhood would fulfill her desires, Anne doggedly searched for a man. "Anyone who would give me attention would be good. I'd have given him my inheritance if it meant a little love and happiness," she says of her desperate search.

She found the attention she was looking for in Mark, whom she relentlessly pursued. "I badgered him into going out with me, I badgered him into telling me he loved me, and I badgered him into proposing. We had nothing in common, but I had someone and that was good enough."

It wasn't good enough, though, as Anne quickly discovered. Her miserable marriage sent her searching all over again for happiness and love, this time on bar stools and dance floors. "If you're feeling lonely in a marriage, going to bars and getting hit on doesn't feel so bad," says Anne.

After three years of emotional abuse, Anne left Mark to move in with a high school friend and her husband. This time she found the longed-for attention in her friend's husband. The two of them planned to leave their spouses, run off together, and start a new life. When he changed his mind, Anne was devastated. "(He) was my out, and instead I was loved again and dropped again." The prospect of happiness seemed more unreachable than ever before.

For the next year, Anne buried herself in bars and brief relationships, and finally moved back home with her parents. She started attending church with her dad, but heard the sermons through stubborn ears. When the pastor's words poked her conscience, she shut him out. In spite of the pokes, though, she couldn't stay away.

One Saturday night, Anne hit the bottom. "I went to a 'Love Sucks Luau' for singles on Valentine's Day. I didn't know anyone, so I felt a little nervous. I drank and drank and drank and drank and drank. The party moved to the apartment of a girl I didn't even know, and I kept crawling to the kitchen to drink some more. I ended up in the bathroom wrapped around the toilet of a total stranger, puking my guts out."

The next morning, Anne lifted herself up from the bathroom floor and looked into the mirror. As she stared into empty eyes, a voice echoed in her drunken head. "Be ye in the world, but not of it," she heard it say. Shocked by the clarity of the words, she looked around to see if someone was there. She saw no one. She looked at her watch. It was 10:30 on Sunday morning, and Anne immediately thought, "I missed church," but for the first time in her life it wasn't a legalistic stab of guilt. "I felt like I *missed* something, like my day was ruined. I wanted to rewind time so I could go."

Whenever we stuff things into the place only He can fill, we lose.

Stunned by her sense of loss, Anne took a long look at her shambled life. Her best efforts had produced only dissatisfaction. Her desperate searching had uncovered only emptiness. She possessed none of the things she wanted most. She *had* missed something.

Anne's desires were legitimate. God placed within men and women the longing to be loved and the need to be happy. However, He didn't create anything in all the world that could meet those needs. Only He can. No amount of kicking and screaming, searching and experimenting, can change the fundamental fact that we need God. We need

Him for *more* than eternal life; we need Him for *this* life. We need Him to satisfy the cravings that gnaw at our souls.

Whenever we stuff things into the place only He can fill, we lose. We trade away the truly valuable for momentary satisfaction. We trade sexual purity for passionate pleasure. We exchange emotional independence for strokes of significance. We give away good health for cultural standards of appearance. We sacrifice spiritual vitality for busy, "productive" lives. Whatever price we pay, it's too much. We miss the blessings of obedience, the rewards of waiting, and the thrill of God's best. Blinded by desires, we hand over our birthrights for bowls of stew. In Anne's words, we "sacrifice little pieces of ourselves to whoever is there to take them."

The beauty of a relationship with God is that He can retrieve all those little pieces of us and put them back together into the persons He designed us to be. He won't necessarily erase the pain of our mistakes, and He'll probably leave the scars from our fights, but He'll envelop us with something we've never known before—the wonder of Him. Anne says it best: "God took the desires I had and replaced them with an overwhelming rush to know Him better."

Solomon—The Destruction of Distraction

During my writing time today, I also accomplished several other things. Between sentences, I made lunch. I ran to McDonald's to buy a Coke. I straightened up the living room, checked the mail, took a nap, read a magazine, signed a birthday card, washed the dishes, and took out the garbage.

When Tammy gets home from work and asks me what I

did today, I'm going to tell her I wrote. It'll be the truth. Sort of. I may not have done it with great focus, but this paragraph alone proves that I *did* write today.

I guess I've been a little distracted, but I've had pretty good reasons. My stomach was growling, so I had to have lunch. It's about 105 degrees at my desk, so an icy Coke was a nice perk. The living room was crying to be cleaned, and the kitchen countertop was a mountain range of dirty dishes. Except for the fact that I didn't enter, I might have won the sweepstakes, so I had to check the mail. After last night's sky-ripping thunderstorm, I needed a little more sleep, and as for the magazine, every good writer stays abreast of current events. Since tomorrow is my friend's birthday, I had to write her card. And the garbage stunk.

It's pretty easy to be distracted (what was I writing about?). Sometimes it's for the best of reasons, and sometimes it's not. No one understands this as well as Solomon.

If ever someone received life on a silver platter, it was Solomon. He grew up the son of Israel's most loved king and the son of his father's most loved wife. In spite of his lower place in the family line-up, he inherited his father's throne, a throne that overlooked a peaceful kingdom on the brink of prosperity. Shortly after Solomon's inauguration, God appeared to him in a dream and issued him a blank check: "Ask for whatever you want me to give you" (1 Kings 3:5).

Whoa! Back up the dream machine! This was *God* talking—ask for whatever you want!? It's not like God does this to everyone. He's never stood at the foot of my bed and made me this offer (although I have a long list under my mattress just in case). Obviously God had something extraordinary for Solomon, and Scripture proves it. He was a smashing success in wealth, wisdom, and power.

- He spoke three thousand proverbs (1 Kings 4:32).
- He wrote a thousand and five songs (1 Kings 4:32).
- He authored three books in the Bible.
- He was a notable botanist and zoologist (1 Kings 4:33).
- He constructed a magnificent temple for the Lord (1 Kings 8:13).
- He brought in twenty-five tons of gold annually (1 Kings 10:14).
- He was greater in riches than all other kings of the earth (1 Kings 10:23).
- He was the most sought after sage of his time (1 Kings 10:24).
- His nation enjoyed unparalleled peace and prosperity.

However . . .

"However" is always the hitch. It's the sure sign that things are not what they seem. It says, "Stay tuned," because the story is not over yet. Two little pigs built destructible houses, *however,* the third little pig built with bricks. Cinderella fled from her handsome prince at the ball, *however,* she dropped a slipper on her way. The Titanic was an unsinkable ship on its triumphant maiden voyage across the Atlantic Ocean, *however* . . .

Solomon's illustrious career pivots twice on the word "however," and both appearances of the adverb indicate that the story is changing.

The first "however" appears immediately after the completion of the temple. For seven years, Solomon had poured his wealth and resources into constructing an extravagant home for God, fulfilling the dream of his father, David. The impressive edifice quickly became the center of Israelite life, their source of national identity. After a long

history of bondage, military conquest, and political up-
heaval, God's chosen people finally seemed to be on the right
track led by a king who had it all. The story was on its way
to a happy ending.

However, when the temple was finished, it took Solomon
thirteen years to complete the construction of his palace.
This was no disaster to put on the evening news, and in
fact, it hardly seems worth mentioning. Solomon *was,* after all, the king, and kings don't live in shacks. Building a
nice palace was certainly an acceptable undertaking for the
world's most reputable leader. *However,* things are not what
they seem. The story is not over yet. The temple was perhaps Solomon's greatest achievement as king, yet he invested
nearly twice as much energy, time, and resources in the
construction of his own palace. "However" hints that
Solomon's life was a little out of balance. His focus had
shifted.

The story then continues with elaboration of Solomon's
increasing splendor. The palace guest book overflowed with
names of the rich and famous from all over the world. The
Queen of Sheba visited the King of Israel and left in aston-
ishment. The lavish wealth and amazing wisdom of
Solomon overwhelmed her.

However, King Solomon loved many foreign women. He
married seven hundred of them and kept another three
hundred around just for fun. The thirteen years he spent
constructing his palace may have whispered that things were
not what they seemed, but this second "however" shouts
that things were all wrong.

It's hard to feel much pity for a man who *chose* to marry
seven hundred women. (Of all the apparent contradictions
in Scripture, this is the most baffling to me: Solomon was
the wisest man in the world; Solomon married seven hun-

dred women.) Friends tell me that being married to *one* woman is a lifetime adventure. Being married to *two* women would seem a severe conflict of interests (not to mention, illegal). Seven hundred women making claims on one man would shred him into unrecognizable pieces.

~

Solomon lost focus, his priorities shifted, and his extraordinary life slowly crumbled.

~

Solomon would know. By the end of his life, the man who built a dazzling dwelling place for the Most High God was erecting altars for the likes of Molech and Ashtoreth. (Molech worship featured child sacrifice, and Ashtoreth was especially pleased with prostitution among her worshipers.) In fact, Solomon built places of worship for *all* the gods of *all* his wives. He may have started out just providing places for them to worship in their own ways, but with the passage of time, he went after their gods, too. He didn't just tolerate them; he pursued them.

And in all of this despicable idolatry, Solomon would have said he still followed God. He still worshiped the God of Abraham, Isaac, and Jacob; he just did it with a lot of distractions (seven hundred to be exact). Some of his pursuits (like building his palace) seemed good, and some of them (like marrying wives numbers two through seven hundred) were obviously bad. In the final analysis, though, it doesn't matter much. The effect was the same. Without a heart "fully devoted to the LORD his God" (1 Kings 11:4), Solomon couldn't keep it all together. He lost focus, his priorities shifted, and his extraordinary life slowly crumbled.

Finding Wisdom in the Folly

Solomon scares me. What happened to him could easily happen to me. While Saul and Esau's stories glare with sin, Solomon's story is subtle. He did good, even great, things. He prayed passionate prayers and vowed whole-hearted commitment. *However*, in spite of his monumental acclaim and achievements, he fizzled into failure. The inability to lock his eyes on the goal and to stay on course was debilitating.

Distractions just seem to happen. I don't have to go looking for them.

I do good things. I can pray with passion, and I readily vow undying commitment. *However*, I glance at the sidelines. I flirt with promising fun. I slow my step and stop to talk along the way. Distractions just seem to happen. I don't have to go looking for them. Some of them are good, and some are obviously bad.

My only hope to run past them is to fix my eyes on the finish line—constantly. Remember Mr. Moore's runners' club? The one thing that kept me pounding down the sidewalk was the thought of home. "Only six blocks to go. This is not fun. Five more blocks. I can do it. That throbbing pain will go away in four more blocks. I think I'm dying, but in three blocks I'll come back to life. This is crazy. I hate running, and in two more blocks I'm done for another day. Home. Home. I can see the house from here. One more block." You get the idea. To keep running, I had to focus on the goal all the way.

I joined the race of faith when I was ten years old, and the goal has blurred several times along the way. On some stretches, peer acceptance clouded my vision. At other places, popularity and success seemed to be what I needed most. More recently, relationships have reached from the sidelines, promising fulfillment if I'll step off the track. Don't get me wrong. Peer acceptance is important, a certain amount of popularity and success is fine, and relationships offer some of life's greatest rewards. But they can never be the goal. If I want to run the race faithfully, I have to run with tunnel vision toward Home. I have to fix my eyes on Jesus, the One who authored my race and is using it to perfect my faith.

Finishing Strong

Fixing my eyes and fighting the distractions requires several things. First, I have to be honest. Regardless of the pious words that roll off my tongue, I know what's in my heart. I know who I am. I am Abraham, desperately trying to help God accomplish His plan. I am Moses, groping for reasons to believe that God has a purpose and plan for me. I am Jacob, playing games with people, manipulating circumstances to benefit me. I am Cain, offering sacrifices out of empty ritual. My motives can be as impure as sewer water in a flooded basement. Admitting these nasty truths is critical because it forces me to see what I am apart from God. Keeping tabs on my depravity reminds me how susceptible I am to sin. I am Saul, Esau, and Solomon all at once.

I find it hardest to focus when I can't remember the last time I talked to God like He was right beside me.

Second, I have to stick to the basics. When my Bible is dusty, I am easily distracted. I find it hardest to focus when I can't remember the last time I talked to God like He was right beside me. I struggle immensely when I'm wrapped up in my life instead of consumed with serving others. Ignoring Bible study, prayer, and service is like sprinting on gravel without shoes and running a marathon after a five-day fast. I'm doomed.

My personal ad reads "SWF worth more than rubies. Running hard in pursuit of You, the perfect God-Man."

Third, I have to control my mind. I can script a novel in seconds. When "he" doesn't call, I instantly know his motive for the crime, five key characters, three chapters of background information, the climactic moment when he is caught (by me, of course), and the story's tearful resolution. The mind is an amazing thing, and oh, so hard to control. I don't have a magic potion to short-circuit brain activity. Instead I have an ongoing struggle to stop the insanity!

Fourth, I have to cling to the truth. I know the stories, I've seen the examples. I've seen faith work for my newfound friends—Abraham, Noah, Moses, Joseph, Jacob, Enoch, Abel, Amram and Jochebed. Their journeys of faith through unanswered questions, intense struggles, and incredible pain paved the way for me. Their footsteps lead straight to the heart of the God who has not changed. He still leaves questions unanswered, pain unaccounted for, and difficulties intact. And He still gives guidance, provides comfort, offers wisdom, and promises peace.

Finally, I have to chase God instead of a partner. I want to get married. I want to have a family. I don't want to do life alone. I also don't want to be in charge of this dream. I'm like a kindergartner in the principal's chair; my perspective is limited, selfish, and immature. On my computer monitor is a card that helps me chase the right Person. It's really a "personals ad" I wrote: *"SWF worth more than rubies. Running hard in pursuit of You, the perfect God-Man."*

The perfect God-Man knows what He's doing. Beyond my comprehension, He pursued me first. Being pursued by an appealing *earthly* someone is exhilarating. A healthy relationship gives strokes of significance, sweetness of companionship, and tons of fun. Take those feelings and multiply by eternity. You've only just begun to discover God's best when you go after the One who came after you first.

Remembering

In the summer of 1988, Dino the dinosaur disappeared. Fred Flintstone left no stone (or pebble) unturned in Bedrock, but he couldn't find his purple pal. Fred did what any desperate dinosaur owner would have done; he took to the airwaves, asking kids across America to help him find Dino. America's young sleuths devoured thousands of boxes of cereal, deciphered the clues inside the boxes, and employed the U.S. Postal Service to deliver their solutions to a disconsolate Fred. "Dino's in Hollyrock," said the kids, so Fred hopped the next flight aboard Transcontinental Terradactyl airline to find his friend. After an exhausting search through Hollyrock, Fred collapsed on the beach to catch his breath. In the distance, he caught sight of a show-off surfer, and as the waves brought the surfer closer to shore, excitement overcame Fred. "Dino! Old pal! I found you!" he cheered, recognizing his missing buddy.

If you missed this news story from 1988, I don't blame you. I almost missed it, too—almost. If it weren't for Padder Dave, I never would have realized there was a crisis in Bedrock. In fact, if it weren't for Padder Dave, I never would have realized that I helped *solve* the crisis in Bedrock.

Padder Dave was my youth pastor ("Padder" was some teen derivation of "Pastor"), and I got to know him pretty well because he was also my writing coach. While wading through reams of edits and revisions, we ate a steady diet of stale chocolate bars, soda, and dry Fruity Pebbles cereal. The experience of working together and winning a national competition was a lifetime highlight for both of us, and one we remembered to each other over the coming years by sending boxes of cereal, bags of chocolate, and other strangely related items.

In the fall of the year that Dino vanished, I received a letter from Padder Dave instructing me to buy the Friday, December 2, 1988, edition of a national newspaper. In it I discovered the Bedrock news, and I also found my name listed among the kids who helped Fred solve the mystery. Unknown to me, Padder Dave had consumed a box of cereal, decoded the clues, and sent a letter with my name to Fred Flintstone.

Padder Dave specialized in memorable reminders, and not just about fruit-flavored cereal and writing contests. His most significant reminder always came in a simple phrase of four words. He scrawled it just before he signed his name to a letter. He spoke it just after "good-bye" in person. "Remember whose you are," he'd say. He could've said, "Be good," or "Make me proud," or "Don't get in trouble," but he went right to the heart of the matter instead. Remember whose you are.

I recently watched the story of a Holocaust victim who

painted her way to survival. A gifted artist, her concentration camp job was to capture on canvas the life (and death) inside the fences. When she finally left the camp, her paintings stayed in the possession of a crumbling Third Reich. While distance and decades separated her from those dark days, her mind, seared by the horror, couldn't forget. Attempting to bring some kind of closure to awful memories, she began a journey to find and reclaim her pictures. Her search led to a Polish museum, but the curators weren't willing to part with such poignant pieces of their history. The paintings are clearly her workmanship, but she'll have to move heaven and earth to own them again.

God moved heaven and earth to reclaim His workmanship. When He created us, He made us His signature piece. Nothing in all creation was made in His image except man and woman. Then we were lost. We weren't just victims left in the ashes of someone else's sin. We weren't just trapped by the corruption of those around us. One by one, we've each chosen to disown our Creator. Every one of us is stained with the blood of our own guilt, doomed by our own depravity.

But God the Creator became God the Redeemer. He embarked on the journey to reclaim His prized workmanship, the poignant expression of Himself; and when He found us, He offered the highest imaginable price to buy us back. The blood of His own Son paid for me, and His resurrection broke the grip of death over me. When He paid the ultimate price, He gave me the opportunity to belong to Him forever. My confession of sin and acceptance of His free gift seals my eternal destination. I will be in heaven forever with Him.

⎯

I am deeply loved and longed for by Someone who is eagerly preparing a place just for me, Someone who can't wait to be with me face-to-face forever!

⎯

I belong to God twice. Revelation 4:11 proclaims His authority in my life because He made me: "You are worthy, our Lord and God, to receive glory and honor and power, for *you created all things,* and by your will they were created and have their being" (emphasis mine). I belong to God because He created me. I am made in His image. Revelation 5:9 echoes His supremacy for another reason: "You are worthy to take the scroll and to open its seals, because *you were slain,* and with your blood *you purchased men* for God from every tribe and language and people and nation" (emphasis mine). I belong to God because He purchased me and *re*created me in the image of His Son.

He purchased me to be part of His Son's bride, the church. In Jewish tradition, when a groom's parents selected a bride for their son, they participated in a betrothal with the bride's family. The betrothal was a binding contract that actually made the pair husband and wife, although they did not live together until the wedding ceremony at a later date. Often the groom gave the bride a gold band to wear as a token of his love. It reminded her that she was loved and that he would come claim her for his own soon. The two then separated, and in the time between the betrothal and the wedding, the groom prepared a home for his bride in his father's house, and the bride prepared herself for their lives together.

I belong to the Bridegroom, and to remind me of the reality of His eternal love, I wear a little gold band on my right hand. It helps me remember that the Father chose me for His Son. It keeps fresh in my mind that when I was ten years old, I accepted His offer of betrothal. It says to me that I am deeply loved and longed for by Someone who is eagerly preparing a place just for me, Someone who can't wait to be with me face-to-face forever! I wear it because it helps me remember whose I am.

Somewhere between the writing of chapter one and chapter ten, a really nice guy claimed my roommate. His name is Jermaine, and he's changed Tammy. She has someone to consider above everyone else. She has someone with whom to share her deepest thoughts and dreams. She has someone she loves to delight more than anyone in all the world. In short, she's in love and plans to stay that way for the rest of this life. On her finger, she wears a beautiful diamond ring to remind herself and the rest of the world that she's taken. She belongs to someone, and it changes the way she lives.

Belonging to the Bridegroom changes the way I live. I may not have a diamond ring, a wedding date, or a bevy of bridesmaids, but I am loved. When I choose to love in return, it affects my passions, adjusts my perspectives, and dictates my pursuits. Instead of wallowing in my "unweddedness," I choose to love Him. When I long to be cherished by a husband, I choose to love Him. At those difficult times when I want to quit the race, I choose to love Him. I choose to love Him because He loved me first. In the security of that love, I can run with perseverance the race marked out for me. The finish line isn't far away, and just beyond it is a wedding feast that'll be worth the wait.

Remember whose you are.

Endnotes

Chapter 2

1. Warren W. Wiersbe, *Be Joyful* (Wheaton, Ill.: Victor Books, 1974), 134.
2. Eugene Peterson, *The Message* (Colorado Springs, Colo.: NavPress, 1995), 487.
3. Wiersbe, *Be Joyful*, 133.

Chapter 3

1. Eugene Peterson, *The Message* (Colorado Springs, Colo.: NavPress, 1995), 6.

Chapter 4

1. Corrie ten Boom, *The Hiding Place* (New York, N.Y.: Bantam Books, 1971), 26–27.

Chapter 5

1. Elizabeth Yates, *Up the Golden Stair* (Nashville: The
    Upper Room, 1990), 48–49.
2. Catherine de Hueck Doherty, *Soul of My Soul* (Notre
    Dame, Ind.: Ave Maria Press, 1985), 58.

Chapter 8

1. Jeffery L. Sheler, "Spiritual America," *US News and
    World Report,* 4 April 1994, 56–57.